PRAISE FOR UNLE

"In *Unleash Talent*, Kara Knollmeyer provides tried and true strategies to bring out the best in all students and staff. Kara highlights the best practice of other leaders in the field while inspiring and motivating through examples from her own passionate educational journey."

—Beth Houf,
proud principal of Fulton Middle School, coauthor of *Lead Like a PIRATE*

"In an education ecosystem where people who don't know our children or our work want to sell us empty grit, catchy quotes, and blind positivity, Kara Knollmeyer knows that people matter most. She knows that you know this too."

—Cornelius Minor,
educator and staff developer

"In *Unleash Talent*, Kara motivates us to dig deep to find the keys to transforming our schools. If you want to learn how to build better relationships with kids and adults and how to value the talent in our buildings, read this book immediately!"

—Salome Thomas-EL,
award-winning principal, speaker, and author

"*Unleash Talent* offers a perfect pause for educators seeking inspiration and actionable steps to finding their own gifts and the gifts of others. Kara brings focus to the importance of reflection and discovery and invites readers to deeply consider their own beliefs, values, perspectives, and talents. Through a combination of inspirational, heartfelt stories and thought-provoking questions, educators become active participants in their reading journey as Kara guides them in a process of finding, cultivating, and promoting talents. Written with sincerity and a commitment to lifting up and celebrating all educators, *Unleash Talent* is a must-add book for any teacher's reading list!"

—Dr. Jennifer Williams,
professor, education strategist, and global educator

"This is an uplifting, inspiring, and empowering book for educators written by an uplifting, inspiring, and empowering educator. In *Unleash Talent*, Knollmeyer takes us on a deep dive into the concept of talent, first defining it in a unique way and then showing how we can use our talents to not only maximize our own gifts but those of others with whom we serve. This is a book that will help readers bring out the best in themselves as well as their colleagues and their students."

—Jeffrey Zoul, EdD,
author, speaker, leadership coach, and president of ConnectEDD

UNLEASH
Talent

**BRINGING OUT THE BEST IN YOURSELF
AND THE LEARNERS YOU SERVE**

KARA KNOLLMEYER

This book is available at special discounts when purchased in quantity for use as premiums, promotions, or fundraisers or for educational use. For inquiries and details, contact the publisher at books@daveburgessconsulting.com.

Published by IMPress,
a division of Dave Burgess Consulting, Inc.

ImpressBooks.org
DaveBurgessConsulting.com

Cover Design by Genesis Kohler
Editing and Interior Design by My Writers' Connection

Library of Congress Control Number: 2018938077
Paperback ISBN: 978-1-948334-02-0
ebook ISBN: 978-1-948334-03-7
First Printing: July 2018

DEDICATION

Mom—

You have believed in me even when I did not believe in myself. On days when I have felt small, you made me feel like I was unstoppable. Your model of love, support, and selflessness has been the guide by which I try to live my life. You have set the bar on how to be a caretaker of talent for everyone around you.

I love you.

CONTENTS

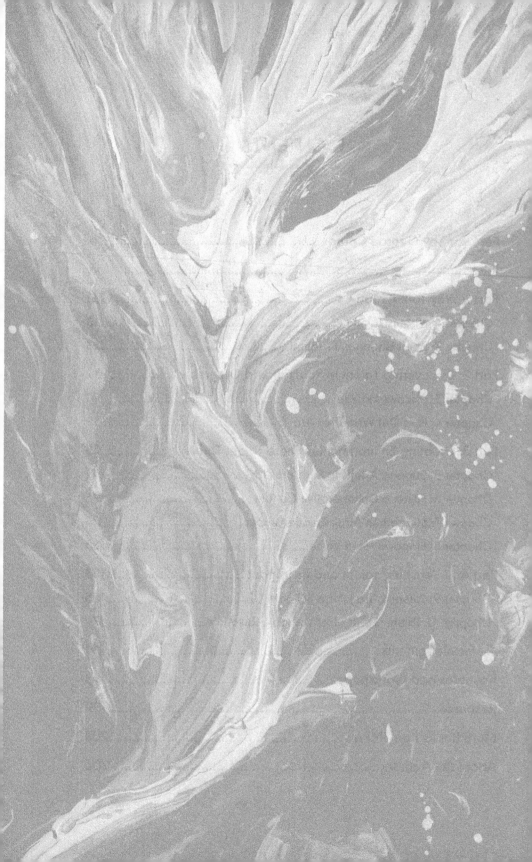

FOREWORD

by George Couros

I **WAS DONE WITH TEACHING.**

Feeling frustrated and that I wasn't making a difference in the work I was doing, I decided it was time to move on and try to find another profession. Although I loved working with students and enjoyed many aspects of education, teaching had fizzled far from passion into a "job." I was ready to quit.

To be honest, if I'd had the opportunity to work somewhere else that year, I would not have stayed in education, nor would I be writing this foreword in a book related to education.

With no other options for money, and due to a number of serendipitous events all seeming to occur at the same time, I was offered a one-year position in a school in a new school district. I remember feeling relaxed and comfortable during my interview for that position. The principal interviewing me didn't barrage me with questions but instead gave me a list of twenty topics we could focus on, and I got to pick. It felt less like an interview and more like a conversation with respected colleagues. We laughed, I cried (seriously), and we talked about things in education that I was extremely passionate about. Things I had forgotten I was passionate about.

I received the job offer a week later, and although I was excited, I still wasn't convinced teaching was for me; in fact, when I had the opportunity to interview for a job outside education *after* I had accepted the teaching position, I called my new principal and told her I had an interview for another job. Wanting to be honest, I told her I wanted to explore the job, even though I was under contract with the school. Looking back, it seems like a crazy move, telling my boss before day one of my employment that I was going to explore another option. I will never forget what she said to me on that phone call: "George, we know we would be blessed to have you, but we also do not want you to second guess taking this position. Take the interview, and if you get it, make a decision that is best for you. If you want to still work for us, we would be very lucky and excited to have you."

I thanked her, hung up the phone, and never took the interview. I knew, at that moment, she was someone I wanted to work for—and I am so grateful I did.

Throughout that first year, I felt trusted, valued, important, and like an expert in the areas that I was given to oversee. There is a difference between *being valued* and *feeling valued,* and I definitely felt valued. I noticed that, instead of rushing home at the end of the day, I would stay after and work on different elements of the school, connect with other staff members, and push myself to learn and get better.

I learned then that, while it is important to believe in yourself, it is much easier to do that when someone believes in you first. So even as I focused on developing my talents and strengths, I started treating my colleagues and students the way my principal treated me. I began to be intentional about noticing and encouraging people's strengths as opposed focusing on their weaknesses. I'm not alone in this. When teachers feel trusted, valued, and important, the way they treat their student changes too.

This quote is tweeted out at conferences all the time, and it drives me absolutely crazy:

"Every child needs at least one adult who is irrationally crazy about him or her."

—URIE BRONFENBRENNER

I want to think about some of the math involved here:
- How many years does a child spend in school?
- How many adults do they interact with?

Based on whatever numbers you come up with for the above, do you really think that "one" (or even five) is enough?

Me neither.

Too often though, when you talk to students about the teachers who have made a significant impact on them, they do not list ten or fifteen, but sometimes only one or two. Even worse, sometimes zero. Obviously, all educators want to make a positive impact on their students, but then we do things sometimes without thinking about the long-term implications on our students. "Response to Intervention" (RTI) meetings are often focused too much on fixing what is wrong with a student instead of on the child's strengths and on what gets him or her excited to come to school every single day.

I'm not saying we should ignore our weaknesses, only that we should start with our strengths. If meetings were periodically held about you and what was wrong with you and how you could be "fixed," how excited would you be to come to work every single day?

Students are no different, and making sure they *feel valued* is a much better way for them to grow.

I'm sure some people disagree with this statement. They offer objections like, "Well, the 'real world' doesn't always value people."

That's true. But my aspirations are not to solely prepare students for the real world. I want to empower them to create a better world.

It is no longer okay for our students to be only able to list one or two teachers that inspired them, as it is no longer okay for educators to be able to list only one or two inspirations in their own career trajectory. This is why I am so excited about Kara Knollmeyer's book. Kara is someone who lives from her passions and wants you to be able to unleash your own. And in so doing, you can inspire and empower others to live from their strengths and passions.

This book is for all educators, school staff, and parents. Kara believes that we first need to support the adults in our school buildings with the goal of helping them tap into their talents so those talents can be used to support students. If you know your staff well and know what their passions are, you can match teachers with students who have similar passions, and the connection can help create strong relationships.

My own passion for bringing out the best in those you serve is mirrored through every word of this book. One of my favorite quotes in the upcoming pages from Kara is the following:

> "Great leaders do not care about showcasing their talent to the entire school. The best leaders use talents to help their staff and students realize how great they are."

The legacy of an educator is not in what *they* do, but what the learners they serve do because of their inspiration, dedication, and passion. As you read this book, you will find practical strategies to bring out the best in yourself as well as others.

I am passionate about what has been written in these pages because I was blessed to have a leader who did all of the things Kara talks about, and she not only changed my career but made my life better as well. I am grateful because in a very short time, I went from not wanting to be involved in education to not wanting to do anything else. One person made that difference. You can be that one person.

When we all focus on unleashing talent together, imagine where our schools, students, and educators can go both as individuals and organizations.

I hope you enjoy Kara's inspiration throughout these pages, and I look forward to hearing the stories of students' and teachers' lives being changed because of the work you have done. Thank you for taking the time to read this, but more importantly, thank you for being the "one" who makes a difference for others. There are people, like me, who will always be grateful.

We develop our talents
first by thinking
we can.

══════════

James E. Faust

INTRODUCTION

I WANTED TO BE AN educator because I love kids. When imagining my career, I visualized my classroom as a stronghold of learning, safety, love, and inspiration where kids could flourish into the people they were born to be. Even in college, I continued to dream about how I would singlehandedly make amazing strides and profound changes, me and my students against the world.

Not until my first year in the classroom did I begin to think about teaching a little differently. I came to three major conclusions: One, teaching is hard! This profession is challenging, and while individual effort is important, collaboration and support are invaluable. Teachers need other teachers, parents, administrators, and others to cheer them on, offer guidance, and believe in their visions. Two, teachers are often at their professional best when helping each other meet their goals. As a collective force, they are capable of affecting powerful and positive change for themselves and their students. Three, teachers and staff members are truly the heart and soul of our schools. I'm all for creating a kid-focused environment, but that approach must always appreciate those on the front lines. Through my experience teaching in both elementary and middle schools, I found that the highest performing schools were those in which the staff performed the best for kids first.

These notions have continued to ring true throughout my career, which has included a variety of leadership roles. Whether launching new teachers, coaching experienced teachers in innovative practices, or heading up curriculum department teams, I have discovered my purpose is to help students succeed by first dedicating and supporting staff. Today I work as a middle school assistant principal in St. Louis, Missouri, and I apply these truths daily because they have helped me become a better servant, leader, and caretaker of talent.

Here's What I Know

Many educators are fond of saying that it's better to teach the whole child instead of simply teaching the curriculum. I would argue this same idea can be applied to a school's faculty and staff. To help educators and other professionals be the best they can be and unleash the talent within them, we must do more than feed them piles of cumbersome data; instead, no matter what our role is, we should shift to focus on our adults as individuals and strive to build a culture of support from all angles. Only then can we be prepared to discover their talents and help our colleagues thrive.

LET'S BEGIN TO ASK . . .

- **Who are our staff members?**
- **Who are their families?**
- **What are their personal passions and hobbies?**
- **What are their personal and professional goals?**
- **What brings them deep excitement and joy?**
- **What are their strengths as individuals?**
- **What are their weaknesses or areas that need improvement?**
- **What talents make up who they are, and how can I unleash them?**

Just as teachers can't effectively teach their students until the students know they care, school administrators cannot effectively lead their employees until those employees know their administrators are invested in their well-being. Our staff members have more to give us than their job descriptions, content information, and curriculum expertise. They have passions, skills, traits, different points of view, and unique life journeys that can enrich an entire school community. Most importantly, the time, care, and energy we put into developing staff members has a direct impact on students' performance in the classroom.

The learners within a school community include every single person we interact with, and how we treat teachers, cafeteria workers, volunteers, and custodial staff. These interactions will strongly correlate with how we serve students. The learners in a school must always include everyone because it takes the power, insights, and talents of everyone to make the biggest impact on students.

Consider your school. Chances are that you have some amazing, untapped talent just waiting to be put to use. School leaders and staff members who take the time to harness the unique talents found at their individual schools are tapping into a powerful resource. I believe educators who support their staff members and work to discover and cultivate their talents will eventually see greater across-the-board job satisfaction, more innovation, and increased retention of effective teachers.

What Is Talent?

Talent is the multiplier. The more energy and attention you invest in it, the greater the yield. The time you spend with your best, is quite simply, your most productive time.

—MARCUS BUCKINGHAM

For the purposes of this book, I will focus on three areas of talent I like to call the T3: the passions, skills, and personality traits that make you who you are. The concept of T3 is inspired by the passion breakdown in the book *Teach Like a PIRATE* by Dave Burgess. The T3 feed your soul. They might even be your trademark. They are definitely something you continually feel a need to improve. Most importantly, I believe that the T3 reach their optimal levels when they are used to serve others.

How This Book Is Structured

To successfully unleash talent, there must be a strong foundation and a solid understanding of what talent is and why it matters.

In Part 1, we will dive deeply into the notion of talent, its intrinsic value, and the importance of encouraging the talents of your school's faculty and staff. This section will show you how to determine your own T3 talents to help you reach your full potential.

In Part 2, we will explore how to cultivate your talent, understand the journey you are on, set goals, and hold yourself accountable. In these chapters, you will learn how to assist others with finding their talents, acting as their advocate, and creating opportunities for them to thrive.

In Part 3, we will discuss the four major actions required to create an environment in which talent can grow: supporting adults to support kids, fostering a collaborative culture, strengthening adult relationships, and empowering staff voice.

In Part 4, we will share ideas, stories, and specific strategies aimed at helping you unleash the talent in your students and in your school community.

Journaling

As a huge believer in reflecting upon what you learn, read, and experience, I carry a journal with me everywhere. When imagining my book, I knew I wanted to embed journaling opportunities in every chapter. I also added specific questions and prompts to spark your thinking. I encourage you to take advantage of this feature, flipping back to previous responses to see how your thoughts are progressing as you read this book. I am giving you permission to write *all* over these pages! If you are reading a digital version of this book, feel free to respond to the journaling in a notebook or space of your own.

Discussion Questions

This book's goal is to help you unleash your talents and the talents of those around you. I included thought-provoking questions at the end of each chapter that will prompt reflection and discussion, whether you're studying this book with a few colleagues, a larger team, your entire school, or a group of social media buddies.

Diverse Voices

I believe in authentic storytelling and looking at education from a wide range of perspectives. To write this book, I reached out to educators, staff, and other phenomenal people who hold a variety of job titles within the field. They are scattered across the United States and beyond, and they all have unique stories and talents. These stories can help us learn from different perspectives of how talent can be unleashed in a multitude of ways.

TALENT OFTEN HIDES IN PLAIN SIGHT, IN THE MOST UNLIKELY PEOPLE AND PLACES. SO LET'S LEARN HOW TO SPOT IT, PROMOTE IT, AND UNLEASH IT ON THE WORLD TODAY!

Who Should Read This Book?

This book is for my favorite group of people in the world: educators. It's for *all* the staff members, teachers, coaches, instructional coaches, classroom assistants, aspiring educators, reading volunteers, curriculum specialists, administrators, department heads, central office workers, and superintendents looking to unleash their own talent and the talent of those around them. This book is for you!

My hope is that this book will shed light on the importance of growing and empowering the whole staff member just as we aim to teach and empower the whole student.

Know this: Talent often hides in plain sight, in the most unlikely people and places. So let's learn how to spot it, promote it, and unleash it on the world today!

PART 1

Why Talent Matters

*Talent is a process,
not a thing.*

≡

David Shenk

CHAPTER 1

What Is Talent?

TALENT IS A TRICKY word, loaded with assumptions. For some people, it's a word associated with the few rather than the masses. For others, it brings to mind laser focus, sacrifice, and hard work. For many, it's simply an intimidating topic best avoided.

Most of us, I would argue, are afraid to recognize and acknowledge our own talents. Sometimes I wonder: Are we more scared of being inadequate or of being abundantly blessed with gifts? After all, when you can blame inadequacy, you can then more easily explain away your failure and lack of effort. When you openly claim your talents, the world expects you to follow through.

Merriam-Webster defines talent as "a special, often athletic, creative, or artistic aptitude," "general intelligence or mental power," and "the natural endowments of a person." I believe talent is all of those things and more. As mentioned in the introduction for this book, I am redefining talent as the T3: the passions, skills, and personality traits that combine to form a unique individual.

What Is Your Trademark?

The T3 make us who we are, and when used for good, they can serve as our positive trademark—the impact we make on the world. When I think of someone who uses her T3 in both her personal and professional lives, I think of one of my closest friends, Alicia. When I think of Alicia's T3, I see her glowing, extroverted personality along with her skills and passion for building relationships with others and hearing their stories. One of the most striking things about Alicia is her uncanny ability to empathetically listen and support others. Whenever I want to share about my day or perspective, she listens nonjudgmentally, which helps me feel validated and important. Alicia always seems to know just what to say when you are feeling down, when you need a boost of confidence, or when you need a laugh. Many people, me included, are drawn to her because of her caring approach. The way Alicia can use and continue to build upon her talents of empathy and active listening helps her be an incredible educator, mom, family member, and friend.

SOMETIMES I WONDER: ARE WE MORE SCARED OF BEING INADEQUATE OR OF BEING ABUNDANTLY BLESSED WITH GIFTS?

Understanding the T3

When viewing talent through this new T3 lens, it helps to firmly differentiate between passions, skills, and personality traits. The table below offers several examples of each category and thought-provoking questions to ask yourself as you explore your own T3. Read on and start learning about yourself!

TALENT 1: PASSIONS

The answers to these questions could be your passions:

- What lights your soul on fire?
- What hobbies do you enjoy?
- What activity makes you lose track of time?

Personal Passions

- Sports/fitness—Baseball, football, hockey, soccer, cheerleading, running, weightlifting, swimming, martial arts
- Art—Painting, sculpting, sketching, graphic design, photography
- Music—Playing a musical instrument, composing music, listening to music, curating music
- Dance—Ballet, tap, jazz, hip-hop, Irish dancing, ballroom
- Reading—Books, ebooks, podcasts, news articles, journals, blogs
- Writing—Journals, blogs, books, articles, short stories
- Nature—Gardening, hiking, walking, exploring, traveling
- Service—Volunteering, philanthropy, good deeds
- Relationships—Family, friends, colleagues

Professional Passions

- Content areas you teach
- Curriculum writing
- School- and district-based committees
- Leadership opportunities
- Building relationships: Colleagues, students, and their families

TALENT 2: SKILLS

A skill is a particular ability that you possess, possibly a mix of soft and hard skills. Soft skills are considered people skills while hard skills are thought of as technical abilities. To succeed in the current digital age and effectively collaborate with peers, a person needs to master both.

Soft Skills

- Emotional intelligence
- Integrity
- Adaptability
- Decision making
- Work ethic
- Reflection
- Proactive tendencies
- Communication
- Critical thinking
- Leadership skills
- Persuasion
- Teamwork

Hard Skills

- Technology proficiency
- Cooking
- Mathematics
- Engineering
- Coding
- Writing
- Keyboarding
- Foreign languages
- Sewing
- Woodworking/carpentry
- Building design

Time Magazine also identified the twenty-one most valuable career skills. See what skills you possess:

Time Valuable Skills

TALENT 3: PERSONALITY TRAITS

Merriam-Webster defines personality traits as "distinguishing quality and inherited characteristics."

The Big 5 ideology, which shows how your personality is displayed in everyday life, states that your personality is built on the following five traits:

- OPENNESS
  - ▶ Inventive/curious vs. Consistent/cautious
- CONSCIOUSNESS
  - ▶ Efficient/organized vs. Easygoing/careless
- EXTROVERSION OR INTROVERSION
  - ▶ Outgoing/energetic vs. Solitary/reserved
- AGREEABLENESS
  - ▶ Friendly/compassionate vs. Challenging/detached
- NEUROTICISM
  - ▶ Sensitive/nervous vs. Secure/confident

Are you curious to learn more about your personality? You can take one of numerous online personality tests to learn more about yourself. If the Big 5 is not your forte, try these tests below. Or if you are like me and just love taking an infinite amount of personality tests for fun, try one or more of the tests below:

- DISC Assessment (discpersonalitytesting.com/free-disc-test)
- Gallup Strength Finder 2.0 (gallupstrengthscenter.com)
- 16 Personalities (16personalities.com/free-personality-test)

Did You Know?

Employers often embed questions related to personality types into their application process to learn more about potential employees and how they would fit into the culture of their workforce.

What's Your T3?

I believe that when we as individuals and professional educators identify and nurture our talents on a daily basis, we will experience more fulfillment and joy at work and at home. As you look through the T3 Talents above, you might still be struggling to find your own. To help you view your talents in this new light and to identify other potential talents, ask yourself some of these questions and jot down the answers. I suspect the results will help point you in the right direction.

- What excited you as a child?

- What do you find yourself gravitating toward in your day-to-day life?

- What do you love to do for fun?

- What would you do if you had one free day with no responsibilities at all?

- Who are the people you admire most?

- What would others list as one of your strengths?

As you ponder your answers to the above journal questions, you must understand how important reflection is in evolving as an educator and a person. Introspection helps you own your unique personalities, strengths, and weaknesses as you navigate complicated personal situations and relationships. This knowledge and ownership will also help you professionally as you collaborate with colleagues or lead staff.

WHAT IS
YOUR TRADEMARK?

The Importance of T3 in a Professional Setting

This year, staff members and administrators at my school, including me, took the DISC Assessment (discpersonalitytesting.com/free-disc-test) to learn more about their work-environment style. Within the DISC Assessment, you can be assessed a combination of the following human-behavior traits:

- Dominant/Direct
- Inspiring/Interactive
- Supportive/Steady
- Cautious/Careful

For example, my DISC Assessment Style is I/CD which means that my approach to work is inspiring, cautious, and dominant. The packet of results you receive upon completing the assessment includes a more in-depth analysis of what your natural style is along with your adapted style based on your specific work environment.

After taking the assessment, we first reviewed our scores as an administrative team to see where our traits lay. We took the time to discuss what information resonated with us and how these behavior-style traits painted a picture of who we are. We also reminisced about how certain DISC traits had played a role in past situations and how they helped us complement one another on the job. Each of our DISC Assessment Styles was different, and we acknowledged that even in light of those differences, we would become stronger together.

Staff members then discussed their results with their teaching teams to learn more about one another. To build upon our work with DISC Assessment, we included time during our staff meetings for each teacher to create a personal User Manual, a how-to-deal-with-me guide for their colleagues. One colleague even described the User's Manual as a "handy guide to get to know me." You could also name it "The Colleague's Guide."

Within each staff member's User Manual, they answered and typed out answers to these prompts (from qz.com/1046131) into a document to share with others:

- My style
- What I value
- What I don't have patience for
- How to best communicate with me
- How to help me
- What people misunderstand about me

We made each of our documents viewable in a folder for all school staff members and encouraged one another to take the time to read them all. See my User Manual here: bit.ly/kkusermanual. Our administrative team went into every teacher team meeting and modeled how to reflect upon these questions using the fishbowl technique. We answered the following questions as an administrative team and allowed the teams to watch us in action. We then provided our staff members time to dive into the User Manuals of others and reflect on their answers to these thought-provoking questions:

- What are the collective strengths of your team?
- What unique traits does each of you have as a team member that help your team work stronger together?
- What are the potential challenges within your team? Where are the gaps? How can you adjust to fill in the gaps?

- What other staff members might your team consult or partner with to support this area of need?
- Are we communicating well with our team? How can we communicate more efficiently with our team members?

While reading each of our staff members' User Manuals, I felt that I was getting a personal glimpse into who they were, which was beneficial in countless ways. Reading and rereading User Manuals helped me understand their communication style preferences and find more ways to better support them instead of merely assuming what they needed.

It's clear the User Manual can be a powerful tool to use with colleagues in many fields. I would also recommend adapting the User Manual to fit your students. Give students a chance to share their interests, likes, dislikes, values, strengths, weaknesses, and more! You will learn more about the individual learners in your classroom while also giving students a chance to learn more about one another. If we provide students with more opportunities to understand themselves and others, they will have a greater capacity for empathy and collaboration, which will only benefit them in the years to come.

Personality Compass with Teams

Another idea to learn more about your staff is to utilize the Personality Compass. If you Google "Personality Compass," you can find countless activities to do with your teaching team, school, or teaching partner. But first, you will want to take the quiz to determine if you are *North*, a natural leader, *South*, a natural team player, *East*, a natural planner, or *West*, a natural risk taker. Scan the QR Code to take the Personality Compass Quiz:

After staff members learn their Personality Compass direction, one great activity I've seen is to have staff members gather with their like-minded colleague in four different spots in the room—North, South, East, or West. Within those Personality Compass groups, individuals can share their . . .

- Priorities
- Biggest strengths
- Weaknesses
- Pace of work
- Motivation
- Traits that might be misperceived by others

From those reflections, each Personality Compass group can share their ideas with others in the whole group. This experience helps paint a bigger picture of how colleagues can best interact with one another.

Another great idea would be to talk with your grade level, department team, or PLCs (Professional Learning Community) to learn how each person helps the group and how they might work against the group. That way, when someone is dragging their heels, instead of asking why Suzie is so opposed to change, they might realize, "Suzie is a South, so she is just trying to make sure everyone is heard before making a decision."

You Are Made of Skills, not Deficits

As you learn more about the T3, you might start to develop biases against some of the passions, skills, or personality traits you encounter; for example, a strong extrovert might view extroversion as a superior talent to introversion. Likewise, an introvert might see introversion as superior. As we all know, neither extroversion nor introversion is better than the other. Each trait is important in its own right. The world needs extroverts and introverts to navigate countless situations and contexts every day. We cannot have one without the other.

The key to overcoming these unavoidable biases is reminding ourselves that we are made up of skills, not deficits. Those traits we and others might perceive as lesser or inferior are indeed important skills. To illustrate, as a natural extrovert, I have seen how I have innately paired some personality traits with my passions and skills. I excel in connecting and communicating with others. It comes naturally to me. People tend to listen to what I am thinking and doing; for example, at my fifth-grade dance recital, during our final performance on stage, we were executing our routine for the very last time. We had practiced our routine hundreds of times prior to this performance, but as sometimes happens, nerves got in the way. I completely forgot the last part of the routine, so I pretended it was over and walked off stage. Without missing a beat, the rest of the team did exactly as I did and followed me off stage. My parents often share this story when they need a good laugh or if they want to reiterate how they always knew I exhibited leadership traits.

Through the years, I cultivated those natural leadership skills and continue to do so daily. My born talent could certainly turn into a deficit if I did not work as hard as I do to evolve within the skillset. From middle school to present day, I have taken every opportunity to grow as a leader. Whether it was signing up for student council as a kid or leading curriculum departments and new teachers as an adult, I relentlessly sought ways to grow and change. As a twenty-nine-year-old school-based administrator, I feel fortunate that my talent and work ethic have brought me to this point. Talent is not realized overnight but tended and nurtured day after day. Remember, you are made of skills, not deficits.

KEEP YOUR EYES WIDE OPEN. THINK . . .

- **What do I daydream about?**
- **What gets me excited?**
- **What do I find myself trying to get better at?**
- **What would I like to learn?**

Stay open to opportunities and become a sponge that soaks up the traits that you and others possess. These qualities that you notice within others and yourself might just be secret talents waiting to be unleashed. Whether or not you are an expert at your talent, if it makes you feel alive, it is worth pursuing.

YOU ARE MADE OF SKILLS, NOT DEFICITS.

We Need All Types of People with All Types of Talents

What we need is more people who specialize in the impossible.

—**THEODORE ROETHKE**

You might view one of your top skills as your most esteemed talent, while others may see a different personality trait or your passion as your strongest talent. If you look deeper into your talents as skills, traits, and passions, you might start to see patterns between all T3 categories; for example, you might see how some of your strong soft skills are in alignment with your personality traits. These soft skills that you excel in might be a key factor for success at your job *and* in your personal life.

Yet sometimes our talents do not have a common foundation or theme. For the record, there is nothing wrong with having a variety of talents that you specialize in; your assortment of traits could help you become an even more well-rounded person while inspiring others to do the same.

A Multitude of Talents

It's your road, and yours alone. Others may walk it with you, but no one can walk it for you.

—**RUMI**

Your school and this world need the talents you have. After all, you are the only person like you out there. Remember: You were gifted with this world, and this world was gifted with you. You have within yourself the ability to make an impact on the people around you. Put another way, your talent adds value to the world.

YOU WERE GIFTED WITH THIS WORLD, AND THIS WORLD WAS GIFTED WITH YOU.

In fact, your colleagues, students, family, and friends need the authentic version of you to help them become their own true selves. Embracing your talents, your T3, can inspire others to do the same. The truth is, the world needs people with a multitude of different talents. Without that diversity of mind, heart, and spirit, our schools, teachers, students, and communities will suffer.

Unleashing those talents is not easy but is necessary for helping others be all they can be. Elisabeth Bostwick, a teacher and speaker in Horseheads, New York, reflects upon how she has learned to unleash talent for the betterment of herself and her school:

Tapping into strengths to unleash talent is a practice we are all capable of developing. For those on the outside, it may appear easier for certain individuals to unleash talent than others. It's often the voices inside our own head that hold us back, and other times it may be that we're allowing doubt from the individuals around us to seep in. I find that unleashing talent occurs when we honor the impact we have and support others to embrace their impact as well.

Teaching is an absolute passion of mine. I'm compelled to invigorate a true love of learning and foster a culture where students genuinely get excited to come to school. I do this by infusing makerspace, project-based learning, passion projects, and technology that empowers student voice and choice within a culture that's rich with trust and relationships. Throughout the school year, these learning opportunities catalyze creativity within students, and their personalities shine brighter each day! I share this with you because in order for my vision to come to fruition, I had to push myself outside of my own comfort zone. While I'm no stranger to developing dynamic experiences in my classroom and sharing ideas with colleagues, early on in my career I faced situations where individuals talked behind my back. This made me feel incredibly uncomfortable. I was isolated by a few who most likely would have preferred that I returned to traditional approaches so that they didn't feel the need to shift. At times, I felt lonely and uneasy. I had a choice to allow those emotions to rule or honor my impact.

Over time, I learned to unleash talent through embracing my why. Your why is the vision behind your life and what matters to you. In other words, your why is your purpose for why you do what you do. Your why can be the spark that helps you get out of bed in the morning. Your why can help you solve difficult problems while being guided by what is important. Your why can help lead you to find your talent.

My why that brings me the most joy is helping others grow and become who they were born to be. I have found that through fully owning and diving into my why, I have had my heart open to many things that have come my way. If I did not embrace my why, I would not have taken the risks or adventures I have taken in my life or challenged any status quo. I have found that by staying true to who you are while living your why, you will inspire yourself with your true potential, but you can be a model for others to follow their own unique paths.

It's imperative that we honor our impact because, after all, our impact has a ripple effect on our schools, families, friends, and community. To foster a vibrant culture, I'm a believer in adding value to uplift others and developing reciprocal appreciation of each other's unique strengths. Unleashing talent isn't something that simply happens overnight but is rather a process that unfolds in our quest to be something bigger than ourselves while contributing to the greater good.

The Bottom Line

If opportunity doesn't knock, build a door.

—MILTON BERLE

To unleash your talents, you must consistently spend more time being open to the skills, passions, and personality traits that you have left to discover. Whether you discover these talents at age three or age eighty, it is your trainability, work ethic, and perseverance—not your born ability—that will help you reach your peak. You have specific talents. You *are* talent. Notice the greatness within you so that you can live your best life—both inside and outside of school.

YOU HAVE SPECIFIC TALENTS. YOU ARE TALENT. NOTICE THE GREATNESS WITHIN YOU SO THAT YOU CAN LIVE YOUR BEST LIFE

JOURNAL

Reflect below on your T3 and the other ideas we have discussed in this chapter.

Personal T3

What are your personal passions?

_____

_____

_____

_____

What are your personal skills? (Soft and/or Hard Skills)

_____

_____

_____

What are your unique personality traits?

_____

_____

_____

_____

Professional T3

What are your professional passions?

_____

_____

_____

_____

What are you professional skills? (Soft and/or Hard Skills)

_____

_____

_____

_____

What are your unique professional personality traits?

_____

_____

_____

_____

_____

What are the common threads between your professional and personal T3? What might this mean? How can you use this knowledge in other areas of your life?

_____

_____

_____

_____

_____

_____

_____

_____

_____

_____

_____

_____

DISCUSSION QUESTIONS

- Do you have any misconceptions about talent? How have these biases influenced your view of yourself and others?

- What's your personal T3? What's your professional T3? How have you used these talents in a positive way?

- Do you consider trainability a talent? Why or why not?

- How can you help your colleagues at school unleash their talent? How would it help you or your team as a whole to be aware of one another's T3?

Put blinders on to those
things that conspire
to hold you back,
especially the ones in
your own head.

═══

Meryl Streep

CHAPTER 2

Don't Undervalue Talent

OUR SELF-ESTEEM AND SELF-CONFIDENCE are such precious entities. If we undervalue ourselves, we are subsequently under-rating our talents as well. By selling ourselves short, we can negatively affect our self-worth, happiness, and peace of mind.

One roadblock to fully appreciating your own gifts is the act of comparing yourself to others. We see others who are successful and receive endless praise by showcasing their strengths, so we naturally want to be more like them; moreover, if we view their talent as embodying the "wow factor," we subconsciously view them as more important. On the other hand, if we do not see ourselves in that same light, we can lock ourselves into a vicious cycle of social comparison.

The truth is that you will never be the best you can be by trying to be someone else. You can emulate the traits you see in those you admire, but the result won't be truly authentic. You were meant to leave your personalized mark on the world. You can only reach your full potential by being who you were designed to be.

THE ROADBLOCK TO FULLY APPRECIATING YOURSELF IS THE ACT OF COMPARING YOURSELF TO OTHERS.

The Comparison Trap

In the current social media and digital age, we have access to online tools capable of connecting us to anyone and everyone. Although social media has brought about countless positive changes, the repetitive use of its many platforms has been found to pose serious threats to mental and emotional health.

In a 2013 study, psychologists at the University of Michigan messaged people five times per day for two weeks to examine how Facebook use influences the two components of subjective well-being: how people feel moment to moment and how satisfied they are with their lives. Their findings are published in PLOS ONE. The authors state: "Our results indicate that Facebook use predicts negative shifts on both of these variables over time. The more people used Facebook at one time point, the worse they felt the next time we text-messaged them; the more they used Facebook over two weeks, the more their life satisfaction levels declined over time."

Connecting with people on Facebook can be fun and satisfying, but too often, we start to compare our lives with the images we're seeing in other people's news feeds. We judge ourselves harshly and find our own lives lacking when, in reality, the contrived and largely artificial images we're seeing on Facebook are only a fleeting glimpse of a person's entire life.

When we scroll through someone's Facebook, Twitter, or Instagram feed, we are passive consumers. We are entertained by content that might or might not be authentic and fully representative of a person's life. Everyone's life, including yours, is far more complicated and diverse than what we allow social media to portray. I like pastor and author Steven Furtick's take on this idea: "The reason we struggle with insecurity is because we compare our behind-the-scenes with everyone else's highlight reel."

When we find ourselves drawn to someone else's exciting, glamorous, and all-around better life, we must stop and take a breath and remember that there are real people with real imperfections behind those images. Instead of comparing ourselves to others, we must remember the greatness that lies within all of us. I do this is by connecting with people on social media on a deeper level, moving beyond superficial interaction to understand who they are, what they're dealing with, and what they have to offer. We all have highs and lows throughout life, and social media might not always accurately represent that. Connecting with others in an authentic manner can help make us all a little more human.

Rather than becoming caught up in the lives of others and your perception of them, remember how special you are. You were born for a reason. You are here for a reason.

CONNECTING WITH OTHERS IN AN AUTHENTIC MANNER CAN HELP MAKE US ALL A LITTLE MORE HUMAN.

Are You Content with Contentment?

Your desire to change must be greater than your desire to stay the same.

—UNKNOWN

Many of us undervalue who we are in various facets of life both inside and outside the school setting. We can get caught up in our mundane routines and forget to snap out of our funk and live life without limitations. Sometimes we default to cruise mode and do only what it takes to get by rather than doing what it takes to thrive.

I stumbled across an article titled, "Don't be Content with Contentment," (bit.ly/whlcontentment) which elaborates more on this idea. Within the piece, the author says:

> *"Likewise, contentment without desire and drive is not success, either. It is complacency. Desire and drive without contentment is not success—it is dissatisfaction. We must understand that contentment, desire, and drive are not mutually exclusive. All three must work together to create true success.*
>
> *If we're only concerned about being content, we can easily settle for less than our best. We can settle for less than excellence. We will not reach beyond our grasp to discover new frontiers through trial and error, curiosity, and innovation. Contentment without desire and drive would keep us in a static state of "good enough." Nothing great was ever achieved through the declaration of 'good enough.'"*

WHAT MAKES YOU, "YOU?"

Chances are, we can all recall a time when we battled feelings of discontentment and dissatisfaction with our lives. Those feelings are normal and part of what makes us human. But we must not stay in that place for too long because it will only keep us from fulfilling our potential.

To break this cycle, accept and love who you are. When you have days of doubt, write down self-affirmations on paper, on your phone, or on a bulletin board in your classroom or office. At my house, I write down self-affirmations on a dry-erase board almost every day. At first, it feels strange to acknowledge your strengths on a regular basis, but over time, you start to believe what you write and say about yourself.

This daily habit has been incredibly beneficial, and I often recommend it to colleagues and students who tend to get trapped in cycles of negative self-talk. Whenever I discover a practice that has a positive result, I make sure to share it with others. I owe this idea to Alexandra Elle, the author of *Words from a Wanderer*, who inspired me to begin a self-affirmation journey almost a year ago. She posts her daily affirmations on Twitter. One of my favorites is, "Today I affirm my worth is not contingent on how others choose to love me, but how I choose to love myself."

Focus on Strengths and Talents

**Reminder: Embrace your T3—
your passions, skills, and personality traits.**

Reflect upon your T3 from Chapter 1: How can you make your strengths even stronger? Focus on your T3 first rather than your weaknesses.

EMBRACE YOUR STRENGTHS AND ALLOW THEM TO WORK FOR YOU RATHER THAN AGAINST YOU.

If we focus on our strengths, we will grow much more quickly rather than diminishing our self-worth because of human weaknesses; for example, if your talent is found in your passion of music, how can you embed this into all areas of your life and school to help you feel more fulfilled? A social studies teacher in our building loves playing music and brings his guitar and amps into school to create and sing geography songs with our middle school students. Not only do you see this teacher's face light up with passion when he is playing his music, the students are overjoyed. When passion is present, it spreads like wildfire to everyone who sees it.

Be Your Authentic Self

Are you living your most authentic life?
How much do you represent
who you are as a person?

In truth, we all probably need to strive for more authenticity. We owe it to ourselves to step up our game as individuals and show ourselves first and the world second what makes us, us. In other words, grow into who you aim to be. Do not shrivel into someone you are scared of becoming. The potential for success can be even scarier than fear.

Author and speaker Brené Brown says, "Courage starts with showing up and letting ourselves be seen." I have found this to be true. Having courage does not mean we are unafraid. Courage is the willingness to step forward even as you're struggling with fear, to push through the fear into what lies ahead. Your authentic self is more powerful than any monster living inside your head trying to hold you back.

To be honest, while writing this book, I was terrified. Although I had wanted to write a book for as long as I can remember, the process of sharing my life and my thoughts with the world was scary. I knew once I published the book, it would be out there, and I couldn't take it back, which was as thrilling as it was nerve-wracking. The worry was constant and included some of the following self-doubts:

- What if I'm not really qualified to write a book?
- What if this book does not have a positive impact on readers?
- What if people don't like it?
- What if they disagree with its message?

Although those fears caused me some distress—and a certain amount of writer's block—I conquered them by living my authentic life. I knew without any doubt that completing my book was more important than my insecurities. These words from renowned scientist Marie Curie helped me put it all into perspective: "Nothing in life is to be feared; It is only to be understood. Now is the time to understand more so that we may become fearless." We must understand what's behind our fears if we are going to conquer them.

I have to remind myself, just as I encourage you, that the talents you bestow on others are more important than your fear of failing or succeeding.

Set Firm Boundaries

Setting boundaries can be especially tough. Pushing your boundaries is even tougher. We see a million things that need our love, care, and assistance, and it's easy to default to "go" mode when we want to positively impact everything.

But this mentality is exhausting, not to mention impossible. Do not get bogged down by things that will not still have an impact on your life in one year, five years, or ten years. Focus on what really matters. When a situation arises, ensure that you are setting boundaries to maximize the impact of your time and energy. Spend more time diving into your T3 and less time wishing you had more time to dive into your T3.

I am just as guilty of this as the next person. I regularly work long hours, morning to night, and often feel I lack the time to dive into my T3, which leaves me feeling tired and uninspired. If I make growing my talents a priority, my attitude is healthier, I am more energetic, and I am more hopeful about what lies ahead. When I take the time to regularly embrace and refine my talents, over time, I become more confident in myself when I see things that once were weaknesses become talents that I am proud of.

To that end, I started writing a daily "Talent To-Do List." We all have lists of chores and errands, but those aren't necessarily things we want to do. The "Talent To-Do List" is filled only with activities we enjoy and that make us feel more alive; for example, on my list, I unleash my T3 passion of helping others by scheduling time within my workday to visit classrooms to help teachers and students with whatever they might need in a supportive, caring, and non-evaluative manner. I know that if I do not make that time a priority, it won't happen. Also on my list is setting aside time to write when I'm at home. Even if I have only fifteen minutes, this is a must. Building upon my passions at home makes me a happier and more well-rounded person and, ultimately, a better wife, administrator, daughter, and friend.

Talent Myths

It is difficult to separate, at times, the myth from the truth.

—**Bob Kane**

You may have seen the image titled "Ten Things That Require Zero Talent." (bit.ly/0Talent) It has surfaced on social media, hit high share counts on LinkedIn, and is a commonly pinned item on Pinterest. That list includes being on time, work ethic, effort, body language, energy, attitude, passion, being coachable, doing extra, and being prepared.

Most likely, the intent of this image was to make us feel we do not need to be innately talented to be successful. But I would argue that this attitude misses the point of what talent is and how it can grow. Here's what I mean:

Being on time, effort, energy, being coachable, doing extra, and being prepared do not just happen in a vacuum. They are skills, and skills must be valued, practiced, and mastered. In time, those skills can become talents. Hard work isn't often viewed as a talent. The famous quote by high school basketball coach Tim Notke, "Hard work beats talent when talent doesn't work hard," furthers this idea. But the truth is that hard work is a skill that takes time, obsession, and commitment. Hard work is a skill. Hard work is also a talent, a talent that sets others apart from those who do not put forth the effort. On the other hand, those who have natural talent but do not put it into action will see others with passion and hard work rise in success before their eyes.

Passion is the key to success. Passion does not need to be separate from talent; the two worlds need each other. Passion does not simply come to you without trying but needs to be explored in order to find success; furthermore, if we have talents but no passion, we lose fulfillment. Passion can be born from experience, energized through practice and interest, and developed into a talent with the proper mindset. Our passions can become the talents that make us unique.

Trainability *Is* a Talent

My best skill was that I was coachable. I was a sponge and aggressive to learn.

—Michael Jordan

This is a pretty powerful message from arguably the best basketball player of all time.

To echo these notions, in the book *The Sports Gene: Inside the Science of Extraordinary Athletic Performance,* David Epstein notes that trainability in exercise is the most important kind of talent, and it may be entirely unrelated with how good you are at the skill. I love this thought because we often view talent and trainability as two separate entities. But what if trainability was *your* talent? How trainable are *you*?

While typing this, the question I just asked even hit *me* hard. I realize that as a person, I focus completely on growing my intellectual and educational skills, but I can lose sight of the physical skill sets I need to build and maintain.

My husband, Adam, is helping to change my mindset on this thought one day at a time. Adam focuses on physical growth and progress more than anyone I have ever met. He loves strength training, specifically the program Starting Strength (startingstrength.com). Within this program, during each workout, you complete squats, presses, and deadlifts along with other exercises as needed while increasing the amount of weight you use each workout incrementally to become stronger.

Adam has spent an endless amount of hours learning about the science behind weight lifting, proper form, and nutrition; His knowledge and persistence in the pursuit of knowledge continues to amaze me. Let me better illustrate this for you: Adam will watch countless YouTube videos and podcasts and read articles. He will take this information to the gym and then execute what he learned while working out. He also videotapes his progress. Through videoing his workouts, he finds ways to improve his stance and form on the spot for instantaneous feedback. His hard work has paid off because he can now deadlift over four hundred pounds!

WHAT IF TRAINABILITY WAS YOUR TALENT? HOW TRAINABLE ARE YOU?

To be honest, when Adam first started training me, I complained, complained, complained about the workout. I wanted to be able to finish the workout in thirty minutes and move on. I did not want to learn the why behind the workout—I just wanted to get it done. One night, Adam finally had a serious pep talk with me. He taught me that in order to learn the proper weightlifting form for my body, I needed to shift my approach and focus on patience in the process. He said that I was difficult to train. This hit me hard. In all other areas of my life, I was coachable, but for fitness, I had a mental block. Adam's words hit me hard, and my train of thought switched immediately because I knew he was right.

If you want to grow in any area of your life, you have to be trainable in order to get there. Mental blocks can detour and even block you, keeping you from fulfilling your wishes and goals. Trainability is the ultimate talent.

Talent is your T3. Your passion, personality traits, and skills are honed and developed over time. Talent does not need to come naturally to be legitimate. You do not become an overnight success by building on your T3. It takes years of determination, practice, and implementation to become who you were born to be. As legendary entertainer Eddie Cantor once said, "It takes twenty years to make an overnight success."

Unleashing Your Limitless Potential

We are often told to dream big and to reach for the stars, but in nearly the same breath, we are advised to be realistic. Being logical is important in many instances, but this world actually needs more people who are *obsessed* with their dreams and passions. People who have dreams that seem unfeasible to the average person. People who can visualize their goal to see the picture of success within their minds. Ultimately people who do whatever it takes to make their dreams a reality each and every day.

Although some may view an obsession with a goal as something negative, obsession with a positive cause is actually a gift. In an article for *Entrepreneur,* Grant Cardone states, "You must be fanatical about success so the world knows you will not compromise or stop. Until you become obsessed with your mission, no one will take you seriously. Until the planet understands you will not give up or go away, that you are 100 percent committed and have complete and utter conviction, you will not get the attention you need and the support you want."

We need people who are not trying to be realistic. We need people who are trying to change the world for the better. And when you are trying to change the world, you do not do ordinary things.

Instead, you commit to reaching for aspirations that are limitless, welcoming failure, never stopping soaking in knowledge, and continually adjusting and adapting.

> ### WE NEED PEOPLE WHO ARE NOT TRYING TO BE REALISTIC. WE NEED PEOPLE WHO ARE TRYING TO CHANGE THE WORLD FOR THE BETTER. AND WHEN YOU ARE TRYING TO CHANGE THE WORLD, YOU DO NOT DO ORDINARY THINGS.

Crabs in a Bucket

When we consistently undervalue our talents, we sometimes find ourselves harboring resentment against those who are making the most of theirs. As the Chinese proverb says, "The person who says it cannot be done should not interrupt the person doing it."

Try not to fall victim to the crab-in-a-bucket mentality. In case you have not heard of this theory, let me explain. Sailors noticed that while traveling across the blue seas and capturing crabs, one crab in a bucket can claw his way out of the bucket successfully with determination. But after the sailors add other crabs to the bucket, all the crabs start fighting and clawing relentlessly to ensure that a single crab does not escape.

In her book *Return to Love: Reflections on the Principles of a Course of Miracles*, Marianne Williamson says, "Our deepest fear is not that we are inadequate. Our deepest fear is that we are powerful beyond measure. It is our light, not our darkness that most frightens us. We ask ourselves, 'Who am I to be brilliant, gorgeous, talented, fabulous?' Actually, who are you not to be? You are a child of God. Your playing small does not serve the world. There is nothing enlightened about shrinking so that other people won't feel insecure around you. We are all meant to shine, as children do."

With this said, just as we can underrate our talents, we do the same to others, either consciously or subconsciously. When we minimize the potential of others, we diminish the leaders and possibilities that could be. When we shut down our possibilities and start believing that it can't be done, we belittle the greatness of others while diminishing our own.

The Bottom Line

You are responsible for the talent that has been entrusted to you.
—HENRI FREDERIC AMIEL

Rather than undervaluing your talents, judging others, making excuses, and limiting your dreams from being too big, be unstoppable! See your talents and dreams as entities that can exist alongside each other, not in opposition.

Welcome dreams that are illogical, for this is the only way we can change the world. As Ann Landers, a former *Chicago-Sun Times* columnist tells us, "Opportunities are usually disguised as hard work, so most people don't recognize them." But you can prove to yourself that you are worth the effort, and you can offer that same gift of empowerment to others, which ends up being the greatest gift of all.

JOURNAL

What are your goals? What are some of your out-of-this-world dreams and aspirations? Which dream is so big and crazy that you even doubt its possibilities?

_____

_____

_____

_____

_____

_____

Think about that goal and write about it here. What steps would you need to take for the short- and long-term to reach this goal?

_____

_____

_____

_____

_____

_____

DISCUSSION QUESTIONS

- Have you ever caught yourself comparing your strengths to the strengths of others in the workplace? How did you turn this into a learning opportunity?

- How can you begin a Talent To-Do List to build in time within your week to grow your T3?

- Friendly competition can be a force of change in and out of work. How has friendly competition pushed you to be a better educator with your colleagues?

- When you catch yourself and others embodying the crab-in-the-bucket mentality, what action can you take to shift to a more positive and welcoming frame of mind?

PART 2

Discovering Talent in Yourself and Others

Everything that you want to be, you already are, and you're simply on the path to discovering it.

≡

Alicia Keys

CHAPTER 3

Discovering You

TIME AND TIME AGAIN, I find our relationship with ourselves directly impacts how we conduct relationships with others. If we do not know our true selves, it will be nearly impossible to help others do the same. Similarly, if we are not aware of our talents—our passions, skills, and personality traits—we will never be in a position to unleash them.

The Chain of Discovery

Discover YOU

V

Discover Your Talents

V

Help Colleagues Discover Who They Are

V

Help Students Discover Who They Are

Once we begin to know ourselves, we will more fully benefit our colleagues and the students we work beside and serve. To start, each of us must ask, "Who am I as a person?" and "Who am I as a professional?" Whatever the answers, remember that you are a human being who needs personal and professional self-love and support. Both of these elements are necessary to self-discovery, but I believe the path starts with clarity.

Find Your Clarity

*The more of me I be,
the clearer I can see.*

—**RACHEL ANDREWS**

Clarity is the mental sharpness and awakening of knowledge. Clarity equals clearness. When you have clarity, you have understanding. Clarity is essential because without it, our view is obscured, our understanding incomplete. When we act without clarity, our decisions are often misguided.

The truth is, I do not think you can gain full clarity 100 percent of the time. Life can be unexpected with many twists and turns that can obstruct your view of the path ahead. But we can practice certain strategies to be more in tune with who we are.

In one of her videos about goal setting, author and life coach Marie Forleo perfectly describes how I have always felt about following your heart. One of the best mantras that Marie lives by is "Clarity comes from engagement, not thought." In other words, until you put something into action and *try*, you will never have clarity if you are making the right decision. No truer words have ever been spoken.

Confession: As you might have noticed, I tend to live inside my head, constantly juggling different thoughts and case scenarios that run through my subconscious brain. As a result, I sometimes lie awake at night, attempting to solve the world's problems.

Oddly enough, I have discovered that if I stop thinking and start doing, I find more resolution. As Jon Gordon says in *The Carpenter,* "Challenges are just part of the journey. There's no accomplishment without struggle. No triumph without test and failures along the way."

Another way to look at this is, until you act and put your thoughts into motion, you might as well worry your life away because your mind alone cannot prepare you for life. Only your action and experience can accomplish that. Failures happen every single day, but how you respond to those failures defines who you are and who you will become.

Give Yourself a Fresh Slate

Sometimes I succeed, sometimes I fail, but every day is a clean slate and a fresh opportunity.

— **GRETCHEN RUBIN**

As you begin to think about gaining clarity, it's easy to catch a case of the dreaded "I-wish-I-hads"—an angst-filled preoccupation with everything you failed to accomplish this school year or the year before. You find yourself thinking:

- I wish I had tried _____
  (add in the curriculum idea here).
- I wish I had been a better _____
  (add in job title here).
- I wish I had taken more risks in the classroom for my students.
- I wish I had built more positive relationships with my colleagues.
- I wish I had been more generous with my love and time to others.

Let's be honest: Most of us start the school year with high hopes and a long list of carefully planned projects, lessons, and classroom improvements. We're committed, excited, and determined to reach all of our goals. But the reality is, the school year moves by quickly, and plans are easily derailed by unexpected events, new policies, and personal limitations. Or maybe just a ridiculous number of snow days. The possibilities that can thwart us are endless, and by the end of the year, we're overwhelmed with guilt about falling short.

But it doesn't have to be this way. I believe we can become so blinded by our elaborate plans that we forget that a new school year actually provides us with a fresh slate. As educators, we have the unique opportunity of starting each day, each week, and each year with a blank canvas. Many other professions don't offer this chance. Instead of dwelling on our past failures and missteps, we have a responsibility to make each new school year better than the year before. Remember this: We can be whoever we want to be today. Who we were yesterday does not have to dictate who we will be today or tomorrow.

REMEMBER THIS:
WE CAN BE WHOEVER WE WANT TO BE TODAY. WHO WE WERE YESTERDAY DOES NOT HAVE TO DICTATE WHO WE WILL BE TODAY OR TOMORROW.

I challenge you to take a fresh-slate approach at your school and encourage your colleagues and students to do the same. Give yourself grace for failures made, and most of all, give that same grace to others. If we can move on from the failures of our past, we can spend less time feeling guilty and more time growing our strengths.

Below, you will see a Fresh-Slate Pledge. I encourage you to sign it, have your colleagues sign it, and adapt it to fit your students so that they can see that they deserve a fresh slate too.

THE FRESH-SLATE PLEDGE

I, _____
(write name here),
**PLEDGE TO GIVE MYSELF AND OTHERS
A FRESH SLATE TODAY, TOMORROW,
NEXT WEEK, AND BEYOND.**

**I WILL STRIVE TO DEVELOP APPROACHES
TO BE GRACIOUS, GIVING, AND CARING TO
MYSELF AND OTHERS. WE ALL DESERVE
NEW CHANCES AND OPPORTUNITIES
TO BE ALL WE WERE BORN TO BE.**

_____

SIGNATURE

Put Your T3 to Work

After you have pressed the reset buttons on any previous missteps, ask yourself, "What are three things I would like to try this year as a person and as a professional?" The idea is to consider your T3, your passions, skills, and personality traits and put them down on paper—or tablet, phone, or laptop—and into action.

Whether you read this book in January or August, it is never too late to set some new goals. You can dive more deeply into one of your existing strengths or pursue something entirely new; for example, while writing this book, I listed my own T3 personal and professional goals for the upcoming school year. Here they are:

KARA'S PERSONAL T3

PASSIONS

Goal: Post a YouTube video about a Sephora makeup haul within the next six months. (I'm a makeup fanatic and have always wanted to do this!)

SKILLS (SOFT OR HARD)

Goal: Increase my strength-training capabilities by continually adding in small incremental weights as I do squats, bench presses, and deadlifts. By the end of next year, I will squat two hundred pounds, bench press one hundred and five pounds, and deadlift two hundred and seventy-five pounds.

PERSONALITY TRAITS

Goal: To capitalize on my outgoing personality, I will challenge myself in the next year to attend more educational networking events and conferences. While there, I will aim to connect with educators and people that I do not know to build new and meaningful connections.

KARA'S PROFESSIONAL T3

PASSIONS

Goal: Write and publish on my blog at least once a week and continue to connect with readers by responding to their comments.

SKILLS (SOFT OR HARD)

Goal: Hone my time management at work. Spend more time with my family than I do on work activities. Adhere to a firm 8 p.m. deadline for all work tasks, putting them aside whether completed or not.

PERSONALITY TRAITS

Goal: Spend less time second-guessing myself next school year. Ask a colleague to serve as my accountability partner and cheer me on when I am in need of reassurance.

Now It's Your Turn

List your own T3 personal and professional goals on the form below. Remember to consider not only your recognizable talents but those passions, skills, and personality traits you are still developing into strengths. And don't forget to add the small steps—accountability and timeline—necessary to reach each of your goals.

PERSONAL T3

PASSIONS

Goal: _____

_____

_____

_____

_____

SKILLS (SOFT OR HARD)

Goal: _____

_____

_____

_____

_____

PERSONALITY TRAITS

Goal: _____

_____

_____

_____

_____

_____

PROFESSIONAL T3

PASSIONS

Goal: _____

_____

_____

_____

_____

SKILLS (SOFT OR HARD)

Goal: _____

_____

_____

_____

_____

PERSONALITY TRAITS

Goal: _____

_____

_____

_____

_____

_____

Trust Your Gut

Trust your instincts.
Intuition doesn't lie.

—OPRAH WINFREY

Everything I am passionate about, everything I yearn to know more about, and everything I am skilled at doing helps shape the person I am. All of these pieces—my make-up obsession, my passion for writing, and my love for family—tell the story of who I am and who I am yet to be. The work I do is important, but I have learned the importance of seeing myself as more than an educator. I came to realize that I'm a complex human being with the potential to do and be anything and everything I can dream up. So are you! The more you truly know your T3, the more you can be your authentic self, personally and professionally. Those passions, skills, and personality traits are some of your best tools for discovering the real you.

And if you are not ready to dive headfirst into some new passions, don't feel guilty. I give you permission to just dip your foot into the water. Even small steps forward can lead to big victories.

EVEN SMALL STEPS FORWARD CAN LEAD TO BIG VICTORIES.

As my mom always told me, "Your inner self knows more than anyone ever will. Trust it." When you get that nagging feeling telling you to do something, listen to it, especially if it persists. We generally experience more regret from not trying than we do from trying and failing.

Whether you call it your gut, intuition, or a still, small voice, it's an opportunity to listen to and grow an inner mentor. In her book, *Playing Big*, Tara Mohr describes our inner mentor as being the "character inside of all of us . . . that is unburdened by fear and untouched by insecurity, that has utter calm and that emanates love for oneself and others, and that knows exactly who we would be if we were brave enough to show up as our true selves." Our inner mentor can be the key to discovering who we are.

When I was a young girl, I always dreamed of becoming a teacher. Teaching always felt like home. During my elementary school years, I would force my friends to play school with me. My unfinished basement was dedicated as my classroom. I even had my own bulky, plastic, red-and-blue easel, makeshift desks, chairs, and extra papers from school that I dug out of the recycling bins.

Every time we played school, I was the teacher while my friends were the students. This was not a coincidence. My friends asked, "Kara, when can we be the teacher?" My answer: "Well, I am practicing to be a teacher, so maybe tomorrow you can have a turn."

Needless to say, I can count on one hand the number of times I allowed other kids to take the driver's seat and teach.

As I grew older, I could not shake the feeling that teaching was my calling. Once high school graduation approached, I had to make a decision about my next steps. Although I wanted to be a teacher, many outside factors were influencing my decision in a different direction.

Because I was a high-achieving student, people responded to my teaching aspirations with comments such as, "Why would you want to become a teacher? They do not get paid anything." Many individuals even elaborated by saying that I was "too smart to be a teacher." This offended me. Some even believed I should go into the medical field where I could make more money and, in their opinions, become more successful. Although my friends and family members had kind intentions, their input was a huge stressor.

Luckily for me, my mom was my advocate. She pushed me to trust my intuition and encouraged me to let my heart lead the way. My mom did not have the opportunity to complete college and was not able to follow her dream of becoming a nurse. She made it her life's work to provide me and my brothers with a world of possibilities and taught us to see that no dream was too big.

Even with my mom's support, I decided to put my teaching aspirations behind me and focus on the medical field. A year into the program, I became increasingly restless and felt unfulfilled. I could not escape this feeling, no matter what I did. Although I was at the top of my class, my subconscious mind was confirming the fact that I was not where I belonged.

After some powerful moments of clarity, I decided to follow my passion. I changed course and resolved to chase my dream of being an educator and leave the perceptions of others behind. Looking back, I know my gut was spot on. There is no other place I would rather be than in education.

Be Vulnerable

When all else fails or you feel that you need more guidance in discovering who you are, be vulnerable about the process.

If we were honest, we would admit that teaching is hard. Leading is hard. Both roles are meaningful and worth it, but that does not make them any less difficult. We know we love what we do as educators, but sometimes we need more fire and passion to remind us of our why.

Although I believe in perseverance and positivity, I also believe in being authentic. Embedding our T3 in the workplace is not always seamless. Some of the tough stories that we are coping with as educators and leaders can weigh us down if we do not have the opportunity to share them.

Sometimes a positive and tenacious spirit can be the best attribute, but it can also be your Achilles heel. To illustrate, one of my T3 personality traits is positivity. I am conscious of the energy I bring into a space and want to leave the space and the people there more uplifted than they were before. I think many educators can relate to the idea that we sometimes assume that if we are usually positive, we cannot open up and share our struggles. By sharing something negative, that also makes us negative. We are also hesitant to share our pitfalls because we don't want to place that burden on someone else, so to avoid this, we handle it ourselves.

But educators need to lean on each other through the good and the bad. I know from experience that it's incredibly difficult to struggle through a problem by yourself. We all need someone to go to, a support team, or a trusted friend. Sharing your tough stories with others isn't weakness. It's what makes us real. It's a way of revealing that authentic self we are all working to discover.

It is beautiful to share the successes of your day and what is going right. I would argue that it's just as beautiful to share what's going wrong. Author Zora Neale Hurston told us, "There is no greater agony than bearing an untold story inside you." We often shared that quote with our students, but I believe it's just as true for teachers and administrators. We all have difficult days, and we must not be afraid to be vulnerable.

Being reflective is a huge part of finding our stories. Jennifer Casa-Todd, teacher, librarian, and author of *Social LEADia* shares how coming to a better understanding of herself has helped her be more patient and understanding of others as well:

> *I have always been ultra-reflective. I am constantly trying to be better and do better. I always aim high, and as a result, my expectations are high as well. I think this has led me to becoming a better teacher and leader, but it has also contributed to alienating people as well.*

> *George Couros, in his book* The Innovator's Mindset, *talks about leading people from their point A to their point B. That was a huge Aha moment for me. I recognized that in all aspects of my life, I had a vision for how I wanted things to go, and I was trying to get people there. I should have maintained that vision and helped them to get there by being more patient and flexible. Knowing this about myself has made an incredible difference to my leadership style and the development of relationships with people. It has actually*

helped me to move learning further because people were no longer intimidated by me. It's an important lesson I take with me when I work with teachers, administrators, parents, and students (as well as my own family!).

For example, I firmly believe that technology should be used to connect students to each other and the world, but I recognize that not everyone is quite there yet. I continue to support and challenge teachers by offering them opportunities to collaborate globally. Last year, one teacher worked with me on a global collaborative project I created, the Amazing Race EDU, and this year, the entire grade-level team is trying it. I was definitely disappointed at first but put my energy in working with the one class. To see it spread this year is entirely worth it. The same is true for so many other opportunities to bring social media into the classroom and connect with others. If I had my way, schools would have open access to all social media, and we would be using it to teach digital citizenship in context and to empower our students to leverage social media for learning and for good. But I know this isn't going to happen overnight. I am grateful for the self-knowledge that has brought me to an understanding that baby steps are fine as long as we are all moving forward.

The Bottom Line

You can't expect to hit the jackpot if you don't put a few nickels in the machine.

—**FLIP WILSON**

As educators and leaders, we are all a unique blend of the personal and the professional. The more we embrace and grow our T3—our strongest passions, skills, and personality traits—the more we gain clarity and become our authentic selves. By putting our T3 into action, trusting our intuition, and allowing ourselves to be vulnerable, we can move closer to being who we are meant to be.

We owe it to ourselves to never give up on the process of discovering who we are. Whether we are twenty-five years old or ninety-eight years old, we have to make a conscious effort to know ourselves. It is a never-ending and beautiful quest and allows us to help others embark on their own journey.

JOURNAL

What makes you feel strong? What makes you feel confident? Reflect and write about these answers to help determine what drives you.

_____

_____

_____

_____

_____

What new personal or professional passions are you interested in trying? What have you tried and failed at? What have you tried and excelled at? What are you afraid to try? What would you pursue if you knew you could not fail?

_____

_____

_____

_____

_____

DISCUSSION QUESTIONS

- Why is discovering who you are as a person and professional the key factor in personal fulfillment? How does this assist you in serving others better?

- Reflect on the T3 personal and professional goals you listed. Which of those goals terrifies you the most? Why? How will you stay consistent in reaching your goals?

- How can you give yourself and colleagues more grace when they fail? What would that look like?

- What does being vulnerable feel like to you? How can we build a culture in which people feel empowered to share their story with others? How would we use those moments as opportunities to build up one another?

Balance, peace, and joy are the fruit of a successful life. It starts with recognizing your talents and finding ways to serve others by using them.

———————

Thomas Kinkade

CHAPTER 4

Find Out Who They Are

UNDERSTANDING OURSELVES IS NOT enough. We must be intentional about taking time to understand the people around us. When we learn how to discover and cultivate our core talents—our passions, skills, and personality traits—we are better able to model that self-awareness to others so they can do the same. As educators and leaders, we must always consider ways to help others grow. How are you helping others find, discover, and unleash their talents?

I strongly believe that T3s are at their optimal levels when used in the service of others. When actively serving, we increase our life satisfaction. We feel good about ourselves, knowing that we have made a positive contribution to someone else. When we use our talents to help others grow their skill sets, we leave a legacy to this world that will last long after our time on earth.

Start with a Compliment

A compliment is verbal sunshine.
—**Robert Orben**

I want you to think about receiving a kind message, email, or social media notification that compliments who you are, what you give, or the work you do. How does it make you feel? How does it shift your day? In my experience, a genuine compliment is uplifting. It fills you with joy and reminds you of the positive things you contribute to others.

Scientific research has shown us that compliments are powerful social tools. A 2012 study found that, to the human brain, a compliment can be as rewarding as receiving cash. Researchers concluded that the positive effects and benefits were similar, that people perform better when receiving a social award, and that complimenting someone could be an effective strategy to use with students in a classroom.

As Mark Twain once said, "I can live for two months on a good compliment." I couldn't agree more. One compliment can help you get through the week, month, school year, or beyond! Imagine if we all embedded more real and sincere compliments into our day to lift up our colleagues. What effect would that have on colleagues, students, and our community?

I began leadership roles, tasks, and responsibilities early on in my educational journey. I learned rapidly that finding out who others are and building relationships with them was the key to team success. But sometimes when you first meet people, you do not know where to begin to find out who they are. In Part 3 of this book, I will dive into how to support adult learners, how to foster a collaborative culture, how to strengthen adult relationships, and how to empower staff voice, which will immensely help you and your team become more united. In addition to these crucial foundational themes, I found that to help determine who others are, you begin with finding the positive qualities within them in order to discover further strengths and talents.

During one of my first evaluations ever as a teacher, my administrator made this comment about me. She said, "You are a sponge. I see you soaking in the environments and learning around you and using it in your classroom the very next day to benefit your students and colleagues." I believe that to be a sponge, you need to have a keen eye on the people, places, and things going on around you. Look and pay attention. The same applies to giving compliments. If we want to be able to give compliments to acknowledge who people are and what they provide, we need to make sure we are taking the time to notice.

When giving compliments, I like to use these thought starters. Give it a try and add a few of your own that feel comfortable and natural.

I appreciate how you _____.

Thank you for_____.

I notice that you_____.

You are very talented in _____
area. Your strengths benefit our school community
because _____.

Say, "I believe in you."

Recently, a colleague I evaluate wrote me a heartfelt message and left it on my office desk. She told me I have brought a positive energy to our school and that I give her feedback that she appreciates. She said the feedback helps her feel valued while constructively pushing her to be a better teacher. Hearing her words made me feel worthy as a leader. We all feel self-conscious at times and wonder if we are doing a good job. Her note meant more to me than I can ever express because it confirmed that I was noticed, appreciated, and making a meaningful impact.

Inside and outside of your school setting, begin with compliments. Make people feel they matter. Look for the strengths of others. Notice and ask more about their personality traits, their passions, and skill sets. If we start with strengths rather than weaknesses, we can build up others and magnify who they are rather than unintentionally taking the people around us for granted.

Be the Caretaker of Talent

Talent is pursued interest.

—**Bob Ross**

People who understand themselves inside and out are more apt to be able to find out who others are too. Human connection is the essential piece to life and education. Our compassion for others helps us become better leaders. Leaders do not just want to take care of their talents; true leaders show up for other people to help them showcase *their* talents.

Throughout my career in education, I have held many different positions: department chair, new teacher, district facilitator, curriculum writer, professional development contributor, mentor teacher, technology integrationist, and administrator. Through each of these roles, I have learned that it is never about me and always about them. It's not about furthering my own career. It's about being a caretaker of talent to help others find what lifts them up. Their success is my success. When we help others discover their talents, it doesn't stop there. We must also help them carefully grow that talent, maintain it, and provide it with opportunities to thrive. How do you do this? How do you get started? Here are some strategies for being a caretaker of talent in your personal life and at school:

Help Make It a Great Workplace

As we will discuss more in future chapters, the most important foundation and piece of building talent is having a workplace that is a great place to work. Above titles and salaries, people want a positive, engaging, and collaborative environment that is an enjoyable place to be. Your place of work builds a reputation over time, and the culture that you foster will help determine the talent you will continue to receive now and in years to come. We all—not just the administrators or leaders—have a responsibility to make our workplace an unforgettable place to be, visit, and work at, for all the right reasons. How we invest in our people, above all else, will determine what our school will become for the students we serve now and for future generations.

Look for the T3 in Formal and Informal Ways

T3 talents can be displayed in a person's personal and professional life. If we get to know our colleagues inside and outside of work, we can learn more about their passions, personality traits, and skills that can benefit them and others inside and outside of the classroom.

For example, two of my former colleagues and lifelong friends, Andrea Docheff and Stacy Huffington, lead the Running Club for my former school. After school, we used to run with students, increase running mileage, and plan team building activities to strengthen the team's relationship with one another. Running and the club reminded Andrea of her lifelong dream to complete a half-marathon. Her passion for running and building relationships with kids gave her the motivation to set goals and to fulfill her dream. This year, she completed her half-marathon and had students cheering her on from the sidelines!

We often think of talents with a one-lens perspective but need to remember that talents can represent and show themselves in many informal and formal ways. One way you can begin to unleash talent in others is to start with passion; passion and talent often complement one another. In an article titled "5 Ways to Recognize and Utilize Talent," speaker and author Karl Staib explains the connection:

Having passion for something can quickly expose or develop a talent, and often the talent is what creates the passion in the first place. Another simple test is to look at passion and how long it lasts or in what circumstances it exposes itself. Is passion present only with certain activities or skills another person is using? Or is passion on its own and existing regardless of what that person is doing? It's much more likely a talent being exposed if they are more passionate about a certain activity or skill than on a topic, for instance. Always look a little deeper into passion to see the root of it, and this will hopefully lead you to more easily recognize talents that relate to that passion.

If we learn what our colleagues are passionate about, we can help them bring this to light in many ways. Recently on Twitter, I asked, "How do you bring personal passion into the classroom to benefit students?" I was curious to learn how others are using their passions beyond their home. Jessica Bulva, an English Language Arts teacher, responded. "Personal passion: my students! Empowering them and making them feel loved, supported, safe, accepted, and inspired . . . my daily goal!" Jessica's tweet reminded me of my why and what inspired me to jump into education from the beginning. Sometimes we underestimate the most important passions that we have, such as empowering and loving our students. But in reality, that passion is the most important passion we can have as educators.

Realize a Little Goes a Long Way

Investing time in others is the key to success, and a little goes a long way. No matter what role you are in, we all need to take the time to walk around the building, stop by the office, and see staff members and teachers in their element. If we only stay in our little corner, we will not see or understand the incredible things they are doing. If we do not see the talent in others, how can we learn from it? How can we appreciate it?

We often expect administration to provide these opportunities, but I have found from experience that staff members often can make a grassroots effort to begin these efforts of their own accord as well. As teachers, we once began a teacher-to-teacher classroom observation walk-through where teachers could sign up to see other teachers in their rooms. Teachers wanted to view how all staff members in the building were succeeding in their area of expertise: special education teachers, P.E. teachers, orchestra teachers, regular education teachers, and beyond. Teachers were amazed by this opportunity and took away many unexpected skills from others; for example, teachers learned how to embed break brakes used in P.E. in their own classrooms. They learned anchor chart ideas from Language Arts teachers that they could steal for their rooms. They saw the talent in their Art and Orchestra students that they did not normally see in a regular setting. We can learn so much from others, but we must take the time to do so and provide opportunities for it to take place.

As an administrator, I often spend time with my secretaries, department heads, custodians, cafeteria employees, and teachers in their environments to view their strengths and to learn from the work they do. Each time I see others, I am always reminded that so many of our employees are going above and beyond in ways that we do not even realize. The strengths of each of our employees should be viewed by as many colleagues in as many roles as possible. We all have something to give to each other, and there is always more to learn. A little time and a little observation go a long way.

Learning through Trial and Error

Ross Cooper, a supervisor of instructional practice K–12 in Allentown, Pennsylvania, believes that to unleash the talent in others, we must learn through doing while focusing on the journey. Ross shares his thoughts here:

Currently I'm in my fourth year as an administrator (and hopefully, a leader). During this time, to unleash the talents in others, I've learned we must send the message that the thoughts and ideas of those with whom we work can make a difference. This notion starts by shifting our mentality from, 'I can't wait to show everyone what I know!' to, 'I can't wait to learn from others!'

When we believe the former, it's obvious; for example, at various points in time, I've worked with administrators who continually were busy on their phones and/or computers while I was talking to them, disregarded my thoughts if they conflicted with theirs, and poked holes in my successes. Although I did not want to work harder for these people, they have taught me what not to do.

Meanwhile, if we sincerely want to lift up others, we treat each and every conversation as if it's the most important one of the day. While I have room to grow in this area, I do think I have made strides by trying to eliminate distractions (e.g., text messaging) when collaborating, actively seeking to understand the points of view of others, and doing my best to communicate verbally and non-verbally that I respect and value everyone else's contributions.

I've learned that leadership is not easy. And it is often unforgiving, as leaders are regularly under the biggest and strongest microscopes. But through continuous self-reflection, and by intentionally surrounding ourselves with the right people, we can keep on moving forward.

Advocate for Others

Once you see the T3 in others and validate their strengths and talents, it is important to advocate for them. All that I am today is because of the team of people who have believed in me in the past and present and continue to push me to be more. Many people become content with where they are and do not realize all they can be. As caretakers of talent, it is our responsibility as team members to remind people of their potential and to help them see the unseen.

When I see talents being displayed in others, I ask them how they are using their talent to give back to others. I ask them what opportunities, resources, and circumstances need to take place for them to be able to show their talents. Even as a teacher, I see the talents of my colleagues and tell my colleagues and my principals about my observations so that we could leverage their strengths for the greater good as a school. I would also invite other teachers and staff members into my room to teach with me where we could bring their talents and strengths to my students.

We need to showcase the talents of as many colleagues as possible. We often get into a rut where we have the same five colleagues lead and share their expertise with others. Although this is appreciated, we then often lose sight of what everyone else has to offer as well. We cannot think that all our colleagues must be talented in order for them to be leaders. Just like talent, leadership looks different for everyone, and everyone needs an opportunity to lead and to give back in their own way.

When we see the talents in others, how can we give them opportunities to do the following?:

- Take part in book studies in topics where their passion lives
- Team with other staff members with similar and different T3s to create amazing learning opportunities for kids
- Share their knowledge with other teachers and staff members inside and outside of their teams and departments
- Participate in creative professional development opportunities in and out of school
- Share their expertise with other schools in and out of the district
- Encourage our staff to present in conferences to represent our school
- Spread their knowledge online or in blogs
- Connect with other people outside of the education world to further develop their talents
- Take on other jobs and roles in which their talents would be best utilized
- Share their talents with students while learning from the talents that students possess

Everyone Is Gifted

Everyone is gifted,
but most people never
open their package.

—UNKNOWN

Just because a person has not found their talent yet does not mean they do not have one. Just because a person might not seem successful in their current role does not mean they are a failure. To reach people where they are, we must understand their current mindset and perspective. We must approach people out of love rather than judgment. Everyone is gifted, and everyone has talents, but it is our responsibility to help our colleagues and workers find the roles, positions, environments, and opportunities in which their talents will shine the brightest.

The popularity of reality shows such as *The Voice* and *America's Got Talent* has somewhat reinforced the notion that talent is something bestowed on a lucky few. But talent is so much more than that. We have to remember that our personal and professional talents can be displayed in a multitude of ways.

As the United States Senator Chuck Grassley once said, "What makes a child gifted may not be good grades in school, but a different way of looking at the world and learning." It is amazing to see the work we are doing in schools in shifting the way we are viewing student strengths and learning as a whole. We must also continue this shift and change how we view our colleagues too.

Encouraging Talent Encourages You

When we are inspired by the talent of others, what we view can subsequently help us realize our gifts too. Viewing the gifts in others does not make us any less gifted; it makes us better and wiser. Ruben Chavez, the creator of the Instagram inspiration source @ThinkGrowProsper, advises us to "Pay attention to the things you are naturally drawn to. They are often connected to your path, passion, and purpose in life. Have the courage to follow them."

I believe the same applies to helping others find their passions. Anytime I have conversations with my colleagues, friends, and family, my goal is to take away something I can learn about them and learn something as a whole to make me better. When I frame my listening in this way, I am able to put myself in the position to learn more about the talents of others while also being able to learn something in return. Viewing talent, professionally and personally, can help make you and others more well-rounded.

One way you can encourage talent is by offering to be someone's unofficial mentor or to be their mentee. We must seek people in our organization to learn from. Through this, we can see how others are embracing their talent, which will help us better embrace ours. Many schools and business organizations have built-in mentor programs. Some of these programs might be beneficial, but the best learning I have received is from those organic relationships and mentorships that I form and seek out with others.

When I was a teacher, I honed in on the new teachers in the building and found ways to support them, to mentor them, and to be a listening ear. I offered to help them with lesson planning, to walk through my grading practices with them, and shared other tips and tricks I had that I thought would benefit them. Through offering support to others, I learned much more in return. Through helping others grow, I always grew as a result by looking at and noticing the talents that they had to offer as well. I also became more fulfilled as an educator, knowing that I could help give back and validate what others had to offer, as this would always benefit other students and colleagues in our school.

The Bottom Line

We rise by lifting others.

—**ROBERT INGERSOLL**

What you give to others is what you will get back. Your effort in others will not only help them grow but will ultimately help you become the best person you can be. Through this effort, you can also grow in your skill set to coach others while also growing other talents you may have.

Each of our staff members has divine talents to share with the school and world. We often start with how we can build the strength of our students, but we must first start by finding out who our staff members are and what they have to offer. Through creating a staff culture of members that feel fulfilled, empowered, and valued, our staff members will be in the position to foster this same love and care for students and their colleagues.

Each act of love that we commit to in our building has the ability to grow to all members of our school. We must all be committed together to give a little time, energy, and love to our colleagues. We all are gifted; we all have something to give, and we all have something to learn as a result. Let us build up the talents in our adults so that they can be the much-needed models for our students.

JOURNAL

Think about a person with whom you work closely on a daily basis. What are their potential T3, their passions, skills, and personality traits?

_____

_____

_____

_____

_____

What are some talents this individual offers that could benefit their students, colleagues, or you?

_____

_____

_____

_____

_____

_____

Consider this person's strongest talents. Write out a compliment in this format:

I appreciate you because you . . .

_____

_____

_____

_____

_____

This helps our school and community because . . .

_____

_____

_____

_____

_____

When you are finished, share it with your colleague.

DISCUSSION QUESTIONS

- How can you embed genuine compliments into your school day to continue to validate the strengths of others? Which compliment thought starter can you begin to use?

- Name ways that you plan on viewing more of the talents of others. How can you begin to be in more spaces of the building to see more talents that your colleagues have to offer?

- Once you view a talent in a colleague, how can you advocate for them to showcase their talent to the school, community, and world?

- Who is an unofficial mentor from the past or present? How have their efforts shaped you to become who you are today?

PART 3

Creating Environments Where Talent Thrives

Never doubt that
a small group
of thoughtful,
committed people
can change the world;
indeed, it is the only
thing that ever has.

Margaret Mead

CHAPTER 5

Support Adults to Support Kids

I N EDUCATION, WE LOVE kids. We all landed in this profession because of the kids; they are our why and the focus of everything we do. Without our students, we would not be here. No one can argue that our most important goal in education is to be all in for students.

But in that process, we sometimes forget to care for the well-being of our teachers and staff members. We forget that our teachers and staff members are just as deserving of the love, care, and support that we strive to give our students. Their welfare is crucial to overall success. Happy and supported staff equals happy and supported students. Shelley Burgess and Beth Houf express a similar idea in *Lead Like a PIRATE*: "As leaders our ability to do what is best for kids often lies within our ability to inspire, influence, and support adults in our system."

Happy and supported staff equals happy and supported students.

When I think of outstanding staff members I have worked with in the past or present, I see . . .

- Secretaries going the extra mile to build lasting relationships with families
- Custodians building partnerships with students who are struggling in the classroom
- Librarians finding that perfect book to spark a child's love for reading
- Counselors responding to crises by giving all their love to students in need
- Paraprofessionals serving as the support system for the teacher and students in the classroom
- Cafeteria workers taking the time to greet students by name as they come through the lunch line
- Veteran teachers sharing their supplies with new teachers who are just starting out

When you think of the staff members within your school building, what do you see? You probably see love, care, hard work, and dedication. Education demands that staff members, teachers, custodians, administrators, bookkeepers, and paraprofessionals alike bring us their very best every day. That's difficult to do if basic needs are not being met.

All staff members are teachers, and all teachers deserve our support.

I consider all the staff members in our building teachers. Each employee makes a big impact on our school community as they do their individual jobs, and it takes all of us, from teachers to cafeteria workers, to make our school work. And all staff members are teachers, and all teachers deserve our support.

Stand by Your Why

People will lose their way when they lose their why.

—**Michael Hyatt**

Through living and standing by your "why," you become true to who you are while helping others stay grounded in their purpose. Karen Festa, a special education teacher in Narragansett, Rhode Island, is a positive example of someone who stands by her why and helps others stay grounded in the process. She is also a firm believer in supporting educators to support students. Here are some of her thoughts about supporting her students and colleagues:

> *Begin each day with a belief from deep in our core that ALL students can learn. Treat every single student as if they were your own child. Produce thoughts that are fueled through passion and positive energy. For me, my thoughts and actions are brought to life as I dance through our classroom door. My willingness to help and support others comes from a belief that we, as educators, are here in this world to make a difference and no matter what . . . our students need us and deserve the very best we have to offer each and every single day. I accept the uniqueness of every child and acknowledge the fact that there is no such thing as a perfect classroom. I celebrate our unique classroom community because there's no place I'd rather be working than with my students. This is my why.*

As educators, we must always remember our "why." On days when we are challenged the most, our "why" becomes our center of gravity which keeps us grounded. When supporting adults, I am proud to share and confess my "why." I am always willing to help and support educators. I get by with so much help from my friends; why not return the favor? School is like a second home to me. Negativity surrounds us. I admit, I don't like negativity, but I know it exists. It still does not stop me. Maybe some people just need time, or need to be heard, or need to feel loved. We must accept our unique differences and be inclusive. Share the goodness with others and spread joy.

When working with adults, it's important to remember two key things:

1. Be present in the moment. Focus on what's needed and how we can best support one another. I try very hard not to share too many comments like "I've had one of those days before; let me tell you a story."

2. In order to understand others, we need to dig deep and understand ourselves. Take each moment, positive or negative, as a learning experience. There are moments in our lives that drive us to be empathetic and compassionate, and yet they may not have been the most comfortable moments.

We are here for a reason, and working with children is such a gift in this world. Support one another by leading and serving others while fulfilling happiness within our own hearts. We might not be able to turn every negative into a positive. With the help of others and our own passionate drive for education, we can lead, serve, and support others to create a ripple effect of kindness as a joyful leader.

Staff Members Are the Backbone

*Teaching is the backbone
of any modern society.*

—**Unknown**

Our staff members are the backbone for our schools. Our staff members help us achieve our "why." Their care, passion, tenacity, and relentlessness to do whatever it takes for kids become the building blocks for learning.

When we support our staff members, it benefits everyone; moreover, supporting adults will always correlate to happy kids and classrooms. This idea ultimately resembles a healthy marriage and family. When you are married and become blessed with children, your focus always shifts to your kids, and rightfully so. Marriage experts repeatedly advise refraining from putting your spouse second. In other words, children face the consequences in an environment where the marriage is disjointed. But by making your spouse a priority, your children will positively benefit from a happier household where love trickles down and all around. Children see and learn from the models of love and support that are provided to them.

Becca Olave, a contributor at DatingDivas.com, reminds her readers that "Once you are married, your marriage matters more, not less, because now people are counting on you." I believe we should send that same message to our staff members and tell them, "Once you are an educator, you matter more, not less, because now students are counting on you."

When you are a staff member, you become a . . .

- Support system for your students and their families
- Facilitator and creator of amazing learning experiences
- Protector of kids and their human spirit
- Role model of what to emulate
- Community member with fellow students, families, and teachers
- Caretaker of talent for your colleagues and students

Teachers and support staff have countless responsibilities and wear many different hats during the course of one day. Only those in education can understand the beautiful but enormous burden they feel each day. When we fail to support these workers, we risk losing their talent and missing out on everything they would have contributed to a classroom. Passion breeds passion. For teachers to deliver worthwhile experiences to students, they must be able to cultivate their talents in worthwhile experiences of their own. We will not see our teachers' talents bloom until we provide the nurturing environments and experiences they desperately crave.

SO HOW CAN WE AUTHENTICALLY SUPPORT OTHERS?

- Support Adults to Support Kids
- Foster a Collaborative Culture
- Strengthen Adult Relationships
- Empower   Staff   Voice

Teachers Need Other Teachers

As teachers, we regularly have so much on our plates that we can default to living in our classrooms and focusing our concerns on our students and our students alone.

Even beyond that, if we were honest, it is simply too easy to shift responsibility to our school leaders when we see a need in our schools. We sometimes think, *They are paid to deal with the big problems, right? Why do I need to get involved?* or *I have too much on my plate to help with one more thing.*

Having said that, we all need to take responsibility in supporting one another, no matter your role, position, and pay grade. We all are responsible for making a positive impact in our building. We are all in the business of making a difference. On the other hand, empowering people should not mean asking people to take on more roles. Empowering people should mean allowing people to grow into who they are, not who you want them to be.

The administrator influence and support in any endeavor is enormous and cannot be stressed enough. But the truth is, it is not always possible to wait for an administrator to come around and give the support that you and others need. This is not to discount the influence of administration; I am a current administrator myself. But we also cannot expect one individual in one role to be our everything. That is why we need a support system of all our adult colleagues.

Very few bonds are stronger than a staff member or teacher-to-teacher support system. The unity among colleagues, when established genuinely and out of love, is unlike any other relationship. Through building community, you build family. We all can relate to this and see the power of these relationships through our daily lives. My former teaching colleagues were the bridesmaids at my wedding, and even though we work at different schools today, we continue to be each other's sounding boards when we need educational advice or different perspectives.

Whether you work with a new teacher who is just getting their feet wet or a stressed teacher who is struggling to get by or the teacher with family crises at home, each of our fellow teachers need us. And no one better understands what it is like to be a teacher than a teacher.

Connect to the World around You

Once we gain connections to teachers inside of our school building, we must then start seeking connections to teachers, educators, and leaders around the world. The world is becoming smaller and smaller in the best way; knowledge is readily available at our disposal with an online click. In addition, we can gain some of the best friendships, mentorships, and learning experiences for our staff members and students as a result of the connections we build online.

Many online connections have opened countless doors for me personally and professionally. Before joining Twitter, I believed it was solely used for online celebrity gossip and wanted nothing to do with it.

But when I attended a social media conference with Julie Smith, media literacy professor and author of *Master the Media*, I realized Twitter was a tool also used to help connect educators to other educators around the world. After I learned this little fact, I changed my mind and joined Twitter right away.

Being connected has given me the courage to unleash my talent for writing, and I started my blog, karaknollmeyer.com, three years ago. My blog has led to speaking opportunities I never would have dreamed of, and those opportunities have led to jobs, friendships, and experiences for which I am eternally grateful.

ONCE WE GAIN CONNECTIONS TO TEACHERS INSIDE OF OUR SCHOOL BUILDING, WE MUST THEN START SEEKING CONNECTIONS TO TEACHERS, EDUCATORS, AND LEADERS AROUND THE WORLD.

Brent Catlett, a K–12 EDU development executive at Apple in Kansas City, Missouri, has also built a strong network online to benefit his educational community and to connect fellow educators. Brent shares how he uses digital connections to open a world of possibilities for teachers:

All educators have a passion for teaching and learning! In my twenty-plus-year year career in education, the positions I have had started initially with supporting the learning of my students but quickly evolved into supporting, working with, and coaching teachers, principals, directors, and superintendents, or one might say adult learners. Throughout my experiences of working with adult learners, I have been driven by knowing I was potentially helping more students by impacting the skill set of the adults that would be working with them.

One of the core areas I am passionate about is that all educators should be connected and utilize a Professional Learning Network (PLN). In fact, I am currently a doctoral candidate working on my dissertation and will soon be conducting research around how educators are using Twitter and other social media as a PLN. Social media sites can allow adult learners to have 24-7 access to "experts" all over the world that can support their own personalized professional learning that impacts their classrooms and students. I have worked tirelessly in my career to support adult learners having a growth mindset that was willing to fail forward for their students. Often my greatest success in this support with the adult learners has been built on relationships with those people and 1:1 mentoring, encouragement, co-teaching, and coaching. Most importantly though, if I could teach those adult learners how to create and sustain a PLN, I felt like I could empower them with the resources they needed to be successful as educators for their students."

Real Talk

One hindrance to teachers being all they can be is competition. Friendly competition can be an incredible benefit to ourselves and kids. If we see something working for another teacher, it could be the force that inspires us to follow suit. Through these efforts, we continue learning and growing while being positively pushed by others.

On the other hand, there is potential for unfriendly competition. We might see others doing incredible things at our school and think, *I wish I could do that.* Rather than seeing their strengths as a benefit to our school system, we might become resentful and allow ourselves to feel less than who we are. Those insecurities can turn into jealousy, which can manifest as gossip, which is a straight-up culture killer.

REMEMBER:
THERE IS ROOM FOR ALL OF US.

It takes more than the efforts of one individual to transform the school system. It takes every single person. Every single person deserves time to contribute and make a difference. As I get ready each morning, I see the Bible verse, Esther 4:14, that hangs framed in my home: "Perhaps this is the moment for which you have been created." Every time I read this verse, it gives me chills. Any day could be the day you and I were made for. Each day is our opportunity to live our destiny. Each moment we waste judging or resenting another person or underestimating ourselves is time we are taking away from unleashing our full potential.

THINK:
WHAT DO YOU HAVE TO OFFER OTHERS?

In the short animated clip, *Obvious to You, Amazing to Others,* author Derek Sivers shares that he used to see his ideas as ordinary thoughts until a reader once sent Sivers an email positively perplexed, wondering how Sivers came up with such great ideas! Therefore, Sivers asks the question: "Are you holding back something that seems too obvious to share?" What may seem clear as day to you may not be for others; this is why sharing with one another should never be underestimated. Nothing is too small, too simple, or too silly to share. What holds you back may be something that someone out there is waiting to hear. The "obvious to you" idea, thought, or passion could be one of your unique talents to share with the world."

Advice for School Leaders

Administrators, leaders, superintendents, and other influential key players in education need to rethink how they provide learning and professional development to their teams. To support students properly, we must first support our staff members; for example, in our current age of innovation, we are asking teachers and staff members to provide exciting classroom experiences, such as Genius Hour and Makerspace, which require skills many teachers haven't yet mastered. If we want students to enjoy and benefit from these kinds of learning experiences, we must incorporate that training into our teachers' professional development.

Let's break this challenge down into three separate parts:

- Teachers and staff need ample time to dive into the concepts we want them to introduce in the classroom; otherwise, how can we be surprised when they feel misguided?
- To properly teach something, teachers need to experience it first.
- Teachers want to feel that their voices are heard and that their opinions matter.

I suggest we flip the script and begin thinking in a backward design.

THINK:
WHAT LEARNING EXPERIENCES DO YOU WANT TO OFFER YOUR STUDENTS? WHAT OPPORTUNITIES WILL HELP THEM BECOME EMPOWERED, CARING, AND REFLECTIVE LEARNERS AND CITIZENS TODAY AND IN THE FUTURE?

Before asking your teachers and support staff to run and create whatever answer you provided above, try it out for yourself first. Enlist the help of one or two willing teachers and work through some of the kinks to scale the experience to your school's needs. Then, when it's been thoroughly vetted, start incorporating the required training into faculty meetings, morning huddles, and special workshops over an extended period of time. As more teachers master the skills needed to duplicate the learning experience in their classrooms, invite them to lead their own workshops to train their colleagues. When teachers feel confident in their own skills, they are more empowered to share those skills. More ownership will translate to more learning in and out of the classroom.

While creating incredible learning opportunities for kids, many schools around the nation are creating timeless experiences for their adults as well. As a previous mentor teacher and technology integrationist, I always considered the experience my staff needed in order for students to be successful. When implementing Makerspace and STEM tools, I relied on the experience and teamwork of colleagues to determine the best way to support our students.

For instance, we created a team of staff members I called the "technovators." They were willing to test out, try, and develop innovative tools first as individuals and eventually in their classrooms. These teachers helped create systems for breakout boxes, tested STEM tools and gadgets, and presented engaging and powerful takeaways and techniques from their learning to other staff members across the building. Their personal knowledge of the technology and innovation trickled down to their students and colleagues, resulting in greater proficiency among both groups.

Best practices for students often translate to best practices for adults. Not only do we deserve the same opportunities that our students deserve, but we can only understand how to teach better if we become the learners who dive into those same experiences.

If we took on these ideas as our truths, we might . . .

- Improve learning and professional development for countless teachers
- Build more bridges between teachers and students through shared learning experiences
- Transform entire school communities

The Bottom Line

If there is anything that we wish to change in the child, we should first examine it, and see whether or not it is something that could be better changed in ourselves.

—CARL JUNG

If our students are missing transformative learning experiences, it most likely means our staff members are also lacking those opportunities. In education, what we focus on at the top trickles down to our students, for better or worse. If teachers and support staff do not feel supported, that frustration can creep into the classroom and have adverse effects on students. Our staff members need us, so let us revolutionize learning for kids by making them a top priority.

As Professor of Education at the UCL Institute of Education Dylan Wiliam says, "If we create a culture where every teacher believes they need to improve, not because they are not good enough but because they can be even better, there is no limit to what we can achieve."

JOURNAL

Who is a support system for you in your current role? How do they support you?

_____

_____

_____

_____

_____

_____

How do your colleagues help support your T3? How do you wish that could improve?

_____

_____

_____

_____

_____

_____

_____

What is a learning experience you'd like to provide to your students but haven't because you haven't had the proper training?

_____

_____

_____

_____

_____

_____

How do you rely on your teammates for support when you need it? How do you return the favor?

_____

_____

_____

_____

_____

_____

DISCUSSION QUESTIONS

- What is the greatest challenge in supporting other adult learners? What can we do to embed more purposeful time into our days to be there for one another?

- Are you holding back something that is obvious to share? What are you holding back? How can you unleash it to others?

- Who is in your network of teacher friends at your building? How can you show more welcoming and open behaviors to others and find new friends to support along the way?

- Best practices for kids often translate to best practices for adults. What best practice are you doing in the class-room that you could use to support other teachers within their practice?

Culture does not
change because we
desire to change it.
Culture changes when
the organization is
transformed; the
culture reflects the
realities of people
working together
every day.

═══════════

Frances Hesselbein

CHAPTER 6

Foster a Collaborative Culture

YOU MIGHT WORK IN a school with a dynamic culture or an apathetic culture. In each environment, you are the same person, but your love for your job and the kind of teacher or staff member you will become will be different at each school. Culture and relationships can make all the difference within an organization.

On that same note, it is not uncommon for a new school leader, new teacher, or new staff member to want to change everything about the school when they see needed areas of growth. But it takes a collaborative culture to create lasting change and to discover the talents of your team members. That collaboration must be woven into everything we do.

Ramona Tower, an instructional coach in Berwyn, Illinois, shares how she fosters this collaboration among the schools where she works:

As an instructional coach, my job is to cultivate and maintain positive relationships with the staff in my district. I am not assigned to a specific school. The four coaches in my department coach three hundred teachers in eight schools. We try to coach and develop teacher leaders in order to maximize our influence.

I enjoy connecting teachers in order to foster a more collaborative culture in our district. Teachers are often reluctant to share the great things that they are doing in their classrooms. I connect teachers to other teachers down the hall, across town, around the nation and the world. That means I will always highlight everything that is going well.

Coaching is a personal and private process; the challenges that we face are private. When I identify something that a teacher does well or a new skill that they've obtained while I've been in their classroom, I encourage them to teach it to someone else. It usually starts with teaching it to their team, but I also encourage them to share at staff meetings or professional learning days. To teach is to learn twice. From time to time I will cover a teacher's class so that they can go observe and meet with a teacher in one of our other district schools across town. My hope is that these positive interactions will improve teaching and learning for students and teachers in our classroom.

To foster a positive school culture, we must be intentional about connecting our staff to one another, encouraging the habits of positive educators, understanding the challenges of others, and making continued efforts to model healthy support for all members of our community.

Shaping Culture Over Time

In the world of art, sculptors rarely create exquisite statues in one sitting. They mold, shape, push and pull for days and weeks or longer to bring their vision to life. The same work has to happen in a school setting in regards to building a positive school culture. School culture finds success in the long game, not the short game.

A school culture is always in existence, but it takes time—weeks, months, and years—to develop and then to maintain. School culture is not an end result; it is something we have to work at every second of every day for as long as our school exists. School culture is the daily interactions, seen or unseen; the values among people, shared or unshared; and patterns of behavior, intentional or unintentional; moreover, the school culture is its *people*. It takes the efforts of *every single person* in the school to build a school culture that prospers.

As educators and leaders, we each have to take personal accountability for the energy we bring to the spaces we occupy: hallways, classrooms, and every inch of our building. Our values *and* actions have to match up in order for our culture to flourish. Whether or not we realize it, we each are currently setting either a positive or negative tone in our building—*and our people are taking notice.*

Building a welcoming space will begin with each of us having conversations with one another to change the paradigm behind the language and meaning of school culture: How do we view it? What does it mean to us? How do we value it? What do we do about it?

Shaping a positive school culture takes time, consistency, and unity. At the heart of any positive culture is a desire to move collectively toward the future and giving one another grace for the challenges we have and the mistakes made in the past and the present.

A Positive Culture Begins with Positive Educators

A positive thinker sees the invisible, feels the intangible, and achieves the impossible.

—**WINSTON CHURCHILL**

Positive Educators . . .

1. Look for the positive and rid the negative

2. Are fountains, not drains

3. Lift up those around them

4. Are grateful

5. Do not forget about other happy people

6. See life through outside lenses

7. Do not make a mountain out of a molehill

8. Find value in everyone

9. Read regularly

10. Think of each day as another chance to start fresh

My mom is my role model for happiness. She taught me years ago that you do not just have good days; you create them. Throughout the years, her words have stuck with me and helped shaped me into the person I am today. Many people might not realize that positive educators are habitual in nature. Here are ten habits of the many that I have curated to help shape my own mindset.

YOU DO NOT HAVE GOOD DAYS; YOU CREATE THEM.

Important Disclaimer: You cannot just tell people to be positive. That advice will get you nowhere. I hope these detailed examples of positive habits will help you better understand the role of individual attitudes in shaping a collaborative culture over time. Here are a few habits of positive educators:

They look for the positive and rid the negative.

We all experience and see negativity. Sometimes it seems that negativity will do anything in its power to take over our lives. But I have learned that although it would be nice to simply wish negativity away, it unfortunately does not work out like that; instead, to be a force of change, we need to actively focus on the positive and to seek the positive out! I truly believe that what you focus on, you will find. When you do see negativity in your school or in your life, train your brain to do something about the issue rather than venting and sulking. Action and mindset are the only ways to accomplish change.

When I am feeling down, I actively focus on the positive and write gratitude notes to those who inspire me with their love, actions, and talents. By shifting my focus to what's good in my life, I can keep myself from falling into a dark place, and I am able to lift up others.

They are fountains, not drains.

Listen to your inner and outer dialogue. What are you communicating to others about yourself and your values? We need to be aware of the tone, message, and body language we are sharing with others. When I think of fountains, I think of an open and flowing stream of water, never ending with resources. Fountains give water to those who need it without asking anything in return. When we think of people who are fountains, we visualize those who are always there for others and who give their love freely without hesitations.

A drain, on the other hand, only takes in water while giving nothing back. Just as people can be fountains, people can be drains. At one point or another, we have all been drains. When we are in bad moods or have a lot going on in our lives, we can tend to suck the happy energy right out of the room and leave others feeling empty. What is crucial about this conversation is to not feel badly about ever being a drain but instead to be able to recognize when you are a drain and push yourself into a constructive mindset instead.

Are you usually a fountain or a drain? Here are a few important questions to help you be more aware of how you naturally communicate:

- When you are outside of school, do you tend to share more positive or negative stories about your school day?
- How do you speak about other staff members or students in the staff lounge when they are not present? Would your words lift them up or tear them down if they had a chance to hear what you said?
- When you see staff members doing fantastic things for students or others, do you take the time to acknowledge these and share your feelings, or do you overlook them?

They lift up those around them.

I often think to myself, *What can I do to make _____'s day?* I try to be in tune to those who might need an extra lift of love, and I do everything in my power to act on that observation with purpose and care.

One day this school year, one of our counselors, Jaime Finck, could tell I was having a difficult week. She surprised me by sending an arrangement of lotuses in a watered vase to me at work with the note, "Orchids: Artistic, independent, and sweet. They love to laugh; truly optimistic, they see the better in life. They are very wise and seem to understand the world more than most. If you ever meet an Orchid, keep her. You'll never meet anyone like her. Thank you for being you." Her sincere act of love was one of the most thoughtful gifts I have ever received. It is amazing what one gesture can do to boost someone's day, week, and year.

They are grateful.

Cheerful people notice the small things that others around them do to be positive change makers. Try to show your appreciation to others in all they do. Every single person wants to feel noticed, even if they do not show it.

I asked this question on Twitter: "How you do show gratitude to colleagues that lift you up?" I received many wonderful responses, including these wonderful ideas:

- Dee R. Kalman (@STEMinistDee) said, "A thoughtful hand-written note is the best way to show your gratitude. And also sharing your praises with district leadership!"
- Maria Galanis (@mariagalanis) said, "It's special when you see people have your back/well-being in mind. Give a written note expressing the gratitude/ appreciation. Maybe bring their fave coffee or tea."
- Scott Moore (@fortprincipal) said, "By returning the favor when it's needed and ensuring genuine trust is built within the culture of colleagues."

I used to think I didn't need other people's gratitude. I just wanted to be able to show my appreciation to others. I quickly learned that deep down, I craved those same actions in return; therefore, through the years, I have become more open and true to who I am by being more honest about what I need in day-to-day conversations. In my personal "User Manual" that I created for staff, in my "Ways to Help Me" section, I wrote, "Acknowledge when I do something you appreciate." I would have never written that request down even two years ago out of fear of being seen as too needy. Today I know better! Showing gratitude to other people and wanting the same in return is normal and healthy, and voicing that aloud can only grow more gratitude within you.

Feeling gratitude and not expressing it is like wrapping a present and not giving it.

—**WILLIAM ARTHUR WARD**

Give the gift of gratitude. When you show colleagues and students that their time is valuable to you and that they matter, you are more likely to see increased self-worth and positive results from that individual.

They do not forget about other happy people.

When you see a happy person, it is usually not a coincidence. Happy people regularly make efforts to maintain joyful spirits. Do not forget about your happy people!

I have found that some of our best servant staff members are the people we overlook most frequently. These people often seem as if they have it all together and are self-sufficient, but they tend to be the last people to ask for help when they need it. They are the first people on the scene to help in a crisis, the people who always seem to know what to do and say in difficult times, and they always appear to be giving more than they are receiving. We see their strengths, but we must remember they can grow weary over time. The same thing happens to students. When a student consistently behaves, works hard, and performs well, we sometimes forget they need watering too. Your blissful colleagues, students, and friends are often the people who need love the most. Happy people fill up the buckets of others but also crave and need that same love in return.

They see life through outside lenses.

Positive educators do not just understand their lives; they also take the time to think about what others are dealing with in front of and behind the scenes. Positive educators are empathetic. They do not just consider their opinion; they think of the why behind the views and actions of others before making irrational judgments and conclusions.

Sometimes when people are dealing with hard matters in their lives, they tend to take it out on people they are close with or people they regularly interact with. As educators, we often tend to be on the receiving end of this when interacting with families, colleagues, and students. Through my experience as a leader and administrator, I have to constantly remind myself to not take these hard moments personally and instead to stay focused on what their perspective might be.

BE EMPATHETIC TO THE LIVES OF THOSE AROUND YOU AND NEVER ASSUME YOU KNOW THE WHOLE STORY.

I try to stay grounded by staying in touch with what is going on in the lives of others around me. Many people are dealing with abundant hardships in their lives: loss of family, illness, homelessness, discrimination, abuse, poverty, and constant worry about the future. Our colleagues, our community, our students, and our personal selves bring our pain with us wherever we go even if we are not trying.

To illustrate this, during the end of the last school year, students placed many letters in my mailbox. As I was reading through the notes and drying my watering eyes, one card especially hit me like a ton of bricks: "Thank you for understanding the challenges of others and wanting to do something about it."

This student acknowledged a T3 talent within me: empathy. His recognition of my skill set helped me realize that empathy is not what

I do; it is who I am. Empathy is a talent many other educators possess. As educators, many of us naturally have this skill, which helped us gravitate to our profession. But to continue enhancing this skill, we have to give ourselves permission to step outside of ourselves and to be fully entrenched in the thoughts, feelings, and perspective of another person. Be empathetic to the lives of those around you and never assume you know the whole story.

They do not make a mountain out of a molehill.

Stop. Breathe. Refocus. Positive people catch themselves before reaching an oblivion of pure terror and stress. When you feel your heartbeat rising, ask yourself: Will this problem matter tomorrow? In three weeks? In a year? In five years?

All of us encounter personal hurdles outside of school. Everyone has bad days, and we each deal with stressors differently. Be mindful to ensure that your stress does not take the best out of you and others. When we see ourselves or our colleagues struggle, we often think the cure is to work harder to make it better. I am a constant work in progress in this area because, when I need to slow down, I tend to push myself harder.

Hard work and trainability is a talent, but we also have to be mindful of when we need a break to breathe and refocus. Self-care is not an add-on; it is a necessity in the service of education. As the Dalai Lama says, "In dealing with those who are undergoing great suffering, if you feel burnout setting in, if you feel demoralized and exhausted, it is best, for the sake of everyone, to withdraw and restore yourself. The point is to have a long-term perspective." We cannot let our long-term goals be pushed aside because we are not willing to take care of our emotional and physical bodies today.

Regain perspective and move forward accordingly by practicing and promoting self-care for yourself and colleagues. Mrs. O'Daniel, our school social worker, created a self-care Bingo challenge for our staff that promoted the art of taking care of yourself first. When teachers completed each box on the table, they were able to pick up small treats and candy from the Dollar Store. If teachers completed all boxes on the sheet, they were eligible for bigger prizes, such as refreshing water bottles and beautiful candles.

Staff Bingo: Self-Care Challenge

Self-care is not a luxury; it is a necessity. Student Services hopes you will join us in reinvesting in yourself and your family over the break!

Complete a bingo line and earn a prize!
(horizontal, vertical, diagonal, or four corners/free space)
Board Blackout earns a bigger prize!

Have a great break!

Spend quality time with a friend/child/spouse	Draw/color or write a nice letter to someone	Try a new food	Exercise	Be creative! Make something
Go to bed early/sleep in late	Read a book or magazine	Sit silently for 10 minutes	Try something new	Take a nap
Do something nice for someone else	Have a cup of tea/coffee/hot chocolate	FREE SPACE	Declutter something	Make someone laugh
Watch a funny video	Go for a walk/run	Call a long distance friend/family member	Watch a movie	Watch the sunrise or sunset
Do yoga or practice mindfulness	Listen to music	Say no to something you don't want to do	Sing out loud/dance	Give away things you no longer need

What other ideas could you add to your self-care challenge?

Positive educators find value in everyone.

Everyone around you has a strength and personal treasure to share with the world. To discover those special gifts in other people, start by reflecting on these questions:

- What are you thankful for about this person?
- What unique T3 (passions, skills, or personality) traits does this person bring to your school?
- What do you think this person could teach you?
- How does this person improve the spaces they inhabit?

They read and learn regularly.

Find a happy person, and I guarantee you have found an avid reader and lifelong learner. When I meet someone with wisdom to share or work with a colleague or student who has interesting perspectives on life, I always ask them a combination of these four questions:

- What is your favorite YouTube channel?
- What books are you reading?
- What podcasts do you follow?
- What blogs do you subscribe to?

Asking these questions has connected me with many new ideas I never would have known existed. I encourage you to do the same with your own students and staff members. To grow and learn, we must actively seek knowledge, or our thoughts, attitudes, and school culture will become stagnant.

They think of each day as another chance to start fresh.

Positive people do not allow yesterday's problems to weigh them down today. They know each day is an incredible opportunity to begin again with a fresh-slate of limitless opportunities. To have the frame of mind to take a fresh-slate approach, you must shift your thinking from the negative to the positive.

Brendan Fretters, an assistant principal in Raleigh, North Carolina, believes in the power of positivity and says the following:

> Positivity is a significant driver in my professional and personal life. I always look for the silver lining in all situations. The foundations for all of this are genuine relationships. Professionally, as a building administrator, I get to know the faculty on a personal level. Smiles and authentic concern, joy, and caring go a long, long way. Will everyone like this? No; however, I learned years ago that in leadership, you're not going to win everyone over. Do what you know is right and move it along.
>
> This foundation is solidified by listening. When I'm listening to anyone—a student, colleague, friend outside of the work setting, whatever the case might be—nothing else gets my attention, nothing. I'm completely zoned in to what the speaker is saying. So often the students, colleagues, and community we all serve just want the chance to be heard but all too often don't have that opportunity in this. Listening fully provides this while creating a relationship foundation in the process. It's a win-win.
>
> Don't be afraid to smile. Avoid fear of taking a few minutes out of the busy day to engage with others about non-school-related events. At the end of the day, we're all human. The relationship piece is paramount to so much, culture and morale certainly included, and genuine positivity is the cherry on top along with being a core component.
>
> The art of positivity, while listening to what people are going through, can help give ourselves and others opportunities to start fresh by helping them see things in a different light. Every day is a new day and a new chance to be better than you were yesterday.

Don't Be Afraid to Ask for Help

Much more goes into building a collaborative culture than simply asking for help. But asking for help is a wonderful place to start. I have come to understand that to truly serve others, we must be willing to ask for help along the way. When students and colleagues see you honestly confronting your own challenges, they will feel more comfortable reaching out to you for guidance. Allowing ourselves to be vulnerable can empower others to do the same.

It's not easy. Many of us have been taught to equate needing help with being weak or inferior. The truth is, none of us has all of the answers. We cannot do it alone. *We need each other.* I have found that by asking others for genuine guidance, you start to heighten the comfort level between you and your peers. Giving to others can include providing them with resources, suggestions, time, effort, and your heart. It can even be established by asking a question to gather feedback, such as "What would you do in this circumstance?" or "I see that you are really successful with _____. Do you have any tips that you could share?"

EVERYONE DESERVES TO FEEL HEARD, AND IT ALL BEGINS WITH US.

When I started my role as an administrator, I sought advice from staff, secretaries, teachers, counselors, and colleagues. I asked them anything and everything from "What does arrival and dismissal of transportation look like?" to "What can I do to best serve the staff and students?" In a new role, relying on the wisdom of your new colleagues is essential to appreciating who they are and helping bridge the gap of what you know and what you need to learn to be successful.

When you ask for help, it is incredible to see how many people will step up to the plate and surpass your expectations. From the beginning, teachers and staff helped me build schedules, plan for an open house, and spent one-on-one time answering my questions. Since then, many of those same individuals have become comfortable asking me for help.

Pick a colleague you don't usually talk to and ask that person a question or for some insight that could improve your teaching practice. You might be surprised to see how new friendships can build and how your school culture can launch to the next level with one small act. All of these ideas can bind together to help shape a positive school culture.

Build a Collaborative Culture by Asking for Help

"I see you are successful in _____, do you have any tips you can share?"

Ask others for genuine help

"If they feel comfortable asking me for help, I am going to feel at ease asking them for help next time."

Heighten comfort level between peers

Build a collaborative culture where support is the norm

"How are we guiding each other to shine lights of support?"

The Bottom Line

*Love one another but make not
a bond of love. Let it rather be
a moving sea between the shores
of your soul.*

—**KAHLIL GIBRAN**

To build a collaborative culture, we must have the courage to be fountains of positivity, to do everything in our power to better understand the challenges of others, and to ask for help when we need guidance.

Nothing is more valuable than time spent loving and understanding one another; it is the heart of what we do as educators, and it must be the heart of our school culture. A positive, collaborative culture is not created with a single action; it is continuously molded based on the relationships and actions of the people who inhabit it. To foster and shape a culture that will last requires all of us, in our individual roles, making our best efforts every single day. Our teachers, our students, and our school communities are worth it.

JOURNAL

What are you and your colleagues already doing to make your school an amazing place to visit?

What can you do to improve your school culture and make it a more welcoming place?

What is the biggest need for improvement in your school community?

What is something you can do to make your school culture better for students and teachers? "Be a fountain, not a drain" is one of my favorite mantras of all time. How can you add more positivity, life, and energy into each conversation and space you enter?

_____

_____

_____

_____

_____

_____

What strategies can you build into your day to refrain from any drain-like behavior?

_____

_____

_____

_____

_____

_____

DISCUSSION QUESTIONS

- How can we unite together across job titles and roles to help make our school an amazing place for everyone who walks in?

- Who is responsible for shaping a positive and collaborative school culture? How do we help empower the community to share this worthwhile responsibility?

- How can we better recognize the personal and professional challenges in others and be willing to do something about it?

- Sometimes asking for help can feel daunting. What steps do we need to take at our schools to foster a culture in which asking for help and counting on one another is the norm?

A healthy adult relationship is one where both people in the relationship give and both receive. There is a safe and open exchange of ideas, feelings, and thoughts, and all perspectives are considered and valued.

Leslie Vernick

CHAPTER 7

Strengthen Adult Relationships

*A*FTER YOU BEGIN TO discover your talents, who you are, and what you bring to the table, it's important to strengthen your adult relationships. As Eleanor Brownn, an educator and public speaker, once famously said, "You cannot serve from an empty vessel." As we continue to lay the groundwork in Part 3, you will see that creating environments where talent thrives is the most pivotal part of this entire process. You cannot completely unleash talent until a strong culture of trust and positive adult relationships has begun to take form. Community and trust take time to grow.

The act of laying a strong foundation is essential to build up the T3—passions, skills, and personality traits—of your team members. As builders know, without the proper foundation, a house might seem put together on the surface, but it will not stand the test of time. Foundations must be strong enough to hold the other components of the home while also withstanding the elements. A school community with a talent-friendly environment is one that will ultimately survive any number of challenges.

You cannot completely unleash talent until a strong culture of trust and positive adult relationships has begun to take form.

Build Relationships with Staff

In May 2017, I wrote a blog post titled, "How to Strengthen Relationships with Students." As I reflect upon this post, I realize I somewhat missed the mark. Although the piece describes fantastic ways to build rapport with students, I forgot to add that these strategies can and should be applied to adults too. Here's my list:

- Greet and welcome every student.
- Be present.
- Listen and value their different perspectives.
- Get to know more about their families, hobbies, and passions.
- Show what you want to learn from them too.
- Bring out the strengths of every student.
- Empower them to lead and make a difference.
- Be fun; don't take yourself too seriously.
- Be true to you; it inspires kids to be true to themselves.

YOU CANNOT COMPLETELY UNLEASH TALENT UNTIL A STRONG CULTURE OF TRUST AND POSITIVE ADULT RELATIONSHIPS HAS BEGUN TO TAKE FORM.

Greet and welcome fellow teachers and students each day.

There is a reason why "hello" is the first word you usually learn in a new language. Saying hello and greeting one another builds a sense of belonging and comfort among peers and strangers. The word hello helps people feel like they belong.

I once worked with an assistant principal who took the time each morning to go to every single classroom to say hello to each teacher. The gesture of saying hello was not only a great start to the day, but it showed us all that we were valued. I always looked forward to this interaction to help start my day on a positive note. This is also important because if you can see that someone is having a hard day, you can make it a priority to support that adult. Your greeting might keep that bad day from turning into a bad week. Our mood and emotions impact our students. If we go into the classroom in a funk, how can we expect our students to have a good day?

Take the time each day to say hello to every teacher, student, and colleague that you encounter. Whether you say hello in the mornings or take the time to acknowledge every staff member that walks by you in the hallways, remember that every interaction matters. Trust and comfort with others grows through countless mini-interactions. In addition, by making their day, you will truly add more positivity to your own day.

When we build a welcoming school environment, we build a community that gets students and adults excited. Liz Gonzalez, a district PBIS coordinator and education consultant in Bakersfield, California, shares her story of how she has built positive and welcoming school environments:

Having a positive school culture is essential for learning. Building community in the school setting does not occur on its own; it has to be cultivated. Developing effective relationships with parents, staff, students, and the community is vital. As a district administrator, I help support Social Emotional Learning programs. I have seen first-hand the value and importance of relationships. Here are some ways our schools have begun to establish and maintain positive relationships:

- *Teachers dedicate the first three days of school to build relationships with students and parents*

- *Create a welcoming environment on Day 1 that makes parents, students, and staff feel welcomed (e.g., positive signs held by staff as students walk through the school gate "You Matter" and offering handshakes/high-fives)*

- *Taking a genuine interest in students and teachers (intentionally investing time with them)*

- *Celebrating progress*

- *Random acts of kindness for staff and students*

- *Doing a Secret Santa around the holidays*

- *Acknowledging parents for their efforts (e.g., during an awards ceremony for perfect attendance. The parents can also be rewarded with a certificate for encouraging and supporting their students' success in attending school every day—perfect attendance for parents!)*

Every child, parent, and staff member has a story; everyone wants to share their story and be noticed. Listening is a great way to acknowledge others and show that that you genuinely care. Calling them by their first name is a great way to continue the relationship building process. Students, parents, and staff feel appreciated when they are validated by their name and are asked questions (e.g. "How are your kids doing?"). Words have power; use them wisely. Take a genuine interest in everyone that walks through the door. Empathy is probably going to be your best weapon yet! It works wonders. Valuing everyone and being a "caring adult" has the impact to make a change with anyone. Dealing with an angry parent, staff, or student can easily go in the right direction if you start with an empathy statement ("I" messages).

Another great way of bridging the community together is by inviting them to the classrooms and showing them what learning is taking place. Parents who need support need to have a resource. Some of the best parenting resources I have seen in our district are . . .

- *Parent Centers (staffed with a full-time parent liaison)*
- *Parent trainings (Loving Solutions for elementary and Parent Project for upper grades)*
- *Parent University (parenting sessions)*
- *Newsletter*
- *Parent Surveys*
- *Parenting booths at Community Events*

EVERY INTERACTION MATTERS.

Be present.

The hardest thing to do in the current digital age is to be present. With all of the apps, emails, texts, and social media notifications we see through each waking moment, we have been subconsciously programmed to worry more about what is happening digitally than in the present moment. In addition to this, if we add our hectic work days, emails, and phone calls into the mix, it is no surprise that we all struggle with living in the moment.

During an interview with London Real Academy, David Allen, a productivity consultant, said that in order to be present in the moment, you must first give yourself the freedom to do so. He noted that if you allow yourself to "just be" and to leave other responsibilities behind, you can better use your emotions and intuitions to be present and to help guide conversation when communicating with others.

Imagine how many more friendships we could build and people we could better serve if we only gave ourselves the time and the permission to do so. In our calendars, we book meetings, but what if we booked more time to get to know one another as human beings? To help yourself be present while getting to know others, I challenge you to . . .

- **Ask to observe a teacher in their classroom**
- **Request another teacher's expertise in an area where their talents shine**
- **Get to know your colleagues outside of school**
- **During your planning or break time within the day, work and respond to emails in another classroom or space in the building to learn more about what others are doing. I love this idea, as I now have a standing desk that I regularly use to be more present within my building.**
- **Co-teach with another teacher that you do not work with. You can even teach together in the cafeteria, gym, hallways, or outside for a lesson if space is limited.**
- **Meet regularly with other staff members to collaborate outside of your team: secretaries, special-subject teachers, teachers in other grade levels, classroom assistants, etc.**

Let the good work you do be shown in the consistency of your presence, words, and actions each day.

Listen and value different teaching perspectives.

I sent out a tweet with the question, "What do you do to value different teaching perspectives in your school?" The responses I received gave me even more insight to what teachers around the world do:

- Tyler Anderson (@teachjanderson) said, "Focus less on the teaching & more on the learning. What's the impact? If it works, celebrate! If it doesn't, how can we modify?"
- Jennifer Regruth (@JennRegruth) said, "I ask to observe in other rooms in my building!"
- Jeff Kubiak (@jeffreykubiak) said, "Listen, ask, connect, observe, disagree with dignity, share."
- Dr. Jake LeBlanc (@Dr_JakeLeBlanc) said, "Cookie Cutters are for cookies! Or in other words BE YOU!"

DIVERSITY OF THOUGHTS AND PEOPLE HELP MAKE US BETTER AS A SCHOOL COMMUNITY.

It is healthy to be exposed to and to consider different viewpoints. In my experience in leading and teaming up with teachers, I have learned that before you can make progress moving your school culture forward, you need to spend time valuing your people. Diversity of thoughts and people help make us better as a school community. When considering the best next steps for your school, consider the following:

- What is the history of the school?
- How can I help honor that history?
- What is unique about each staff member? How can I get to know who they are?
- How can I better understand the varied perspectives of members of the school and see where each person is coming from?

Learning more about others shows that we value their wisdom. It is not about one individual or a single agenda, because each of our agendas should include nothing else but to better serve others. The truth is that sometimes in our quest to value different perspectives, we puff up our egos and let our viewpoints take priority over other people and their viewpoints. Too much ego will diminish the talent and care we have to share with one another. We have to constantly be aware that we always have more to learn than what we know in any given moment. We will never know all the answers that exist to all the dilemmas in the world, but we can get closer to the answers if we build unity with the people around us.

Get to know more about their family, hobbies, and interests.

As educators, we always revert to talking about how our day is going in the classroom or sharing stories that happened at school. I challenge you to spend more time on other conversations. Take time before school, during lunch time, after school, out of school, or at gatherings to get to know your colleagues personally. Ask about their families, what they do for fun, what they did over the weekend, and the passions they pursue outside of school. If we do not ask those questions, we lose the opportunity to find common ground.

Some of the questions I have asked have led to important friendships; for example, a year and a half ago I posted a tweet asking other educators how they hold one another accountable for fitness goals. I immediately connected with two Canadian educators, Dana Ariss and Megan Valois. I had never met them. From there, we started a Voxer group to post our daily happenings of what healthy foods we ate that day, what workouts we did, and other vital tips. Through this group, we have built a strong friendship. Our Voxer chat began with a focus on integrating fitness into our lives as educators and became an entire support system for friends.

Never underestimate the power of one question and its potential to build connections that you would have never dreamed of otherwise.

Look at every teacher interaction through a nonjudgmental lens.

It is too easy to judge people and ourselves. We see something that a teacher is doing that we would not do ourselves and think, *I would have done that differently. I would have done* _____. Although there is nothing wrong with thinking of ways to improve, we have to be careful about how we view others and our approach to them. Are we looking to judge people or to help them? People do things differently for a variety of reasons. Their approach to teaching might be attributed to their background as an individual, how they were taught as a student, their training as an educator, and what their school valued in the past and the present. Before we judge others, it is important to understand them.

Our intentions matter. People will always have a hard time trusting if they feel they are being judged.

WHAT IF WE LOVED OTHER PEOPLE MORE THAN WE LOVED JUDGING THEM?

Let teachers start over with a fresh slate when mistakes happen.

Earlier in the book, we discussed the fresh-slate approach. Sometimes, we all need a fresh slate. That's why a new haircut can feel so empowering. Fresh slates can make you feel brand new and ready to conquer the world!

People make mistakes every day, and how we, as their colleagues, react to their missteps can help them grow or shrink in value. Being quick to judge, being jealous, or denigrating someone else not only destroys a relationship with a colleague but also spreads negativity throughout a school community.

Be the person who is willing to walk and lead beside your colleagues. The willingness to walk hand-in-hand with someone says more about your ability to lead than anything else. As John Wooden says, "Be more concerned with what you can do for others than what others can do for you. You'll be surprised at the results."

THINK ABOUT THIS:
HOW CAN YOU MAKE TEACHERS' TALENTS
MORE VISIBLE SO THAT PEOPLE KNOW
WHAT THEY CAN LEARN FROM EACH OTHER?

Show that you want to learn from them too.

When is the last time you asked another teacher, colleague, or student, "What can I learn from you?" or "Can you teach me how you did _____?" Showing that you want to learn from others makes you more approachable, caring, and relatable.

Be fun; never take yourself too seriously.

In one of the best YouTube videos I have ever watched, "How to Have More Fun in Your Life," author Matt Weinstein discusses the premise of his book *Work Like a Dog*. He says,

> *"How many times have you heard somebody say, 'Oh man, I've been working like a dog.' But the question is, do you ever take a moment to notice how your dog spends his day? . . . . Dogs don't seem to know the difference between work and play, and everything is fun to them."*

If you have a dog, you know that every time they see you, it is the best day of their lives. What if we lived by this thinking? What if every day looked like it might be the best day of our lives?

Whether I am dressing up in a Clifford the Big Red Dog costume for Read Across America, running around the building on the hundredth day of school dressed as an old woman with my pretend walker, or dancing to the latest tunes, I do everything in my power to not take myself too seriously. When I am having fun, it allows me to loosen up, to take myself less seriously, and to be present. As a result, it helps others loosen up too. After all, life is too short to be taken for granted with the worry of now.

Whose Responsibility Is This?

With all of these thoughts considered, it is crucial to note that the responsibility of these efforts is not solely reliant on the administrator or leader. We must all cultivate relationships with one another: cafeteria workers, paraprofessionals, teachers, teacher assistants, secretaries, custodians, principals, superintendents, and parents. The ownership of unity and improvement should be *everyone's* collective effort.

> ## THE OWNERSHIP OF UNITY
> ## AND IMPROVEMENT SHOULD BE
> ## EVERYONE'S COLLECTIVE EFFORT.

I believe that growing stronger relationships with our colleagues is *the* most important work that we do as educators and leaders. Teaching is one of the hardest jobs that exist. We need the adult support systems in our lives in order to keep us going and to love us through the hard times.

In order for educators to best teach students, they need colleagues who care about them as humans first so that love trickles down to our kids.

But here is the caveat: When building relationships with colleagues, do not do this with the intent to manage them. You are not managing people; you are investing in them. When you invest in teachers and their interests, talents, and skill sets, the return on the investment will always give more to the school community than you can even imagine. Whether you are a child or an adult, everyone wants to feel genuinely cared about; therefore, you can never go wrong by devoting your spirit to those you serve. By doing what you love, you can awaken the hearts of others and inspire them to be all they can be.

Inspire Others

Nothing refreshes the soul more than being around another person who inspires and lifts you to new dimensions. I yearn for these moments of inspiration each day.

I once heard someone say, "Some people do not need to be inspired; they just are self-driven with inspiration." But the world is like art, and art inspires other art. Whether we realize it or not, we are molded from and by the people around us. We also mold other people by our behaviors; people are always watching us and looking at what we do every single moment of every single day. As a result, we grow closer together in our bonds with one another when we can be the catalyst of hope for another person.

5 CHARACTERISTICS OF PEOPLE WHO INSPIRE OTHERS

1. Heart of a Servant
2. Brave
3. Accepting of Others
4. Tenacious
5. Vulnerable

As *Start with Why* author Simon Sinek, says, "The more people you inspire, the more people will inspire you." Each moment we inspire others or ourselves, we can draw ourselves closer to unleashing talent.

Let us use our role as educators and leaders to take these opportunities and make the most of them. Acknowledging how people inspire us can help us build stronger bonds with each other. In no particular order, here are characteristics that inspire others to be all they can be.

1. Heart of a Servant

The best leaders are the best servants. The most inspiring people are the people who love others with all their heart and being. Servant leaders make you feel that they will drop anything at any time to help you and to love you without any expectations. Servants are fountains and not drains; they aim to lift up people as a result of their presence.

SERVANTS ARE FOUNTAINS AND NOT DRAINS.

I work with the best cafeteria manager in the world, Toni Berhorst. She is the epitome of a servant heart. Toni wants all students and adults to feel supported and takes personal responsibility for making a difference in our school. When she sees students sitting alone at breakfast or upset at lunch, Toni takes every opportunity to show those students she values them. She seeks ways to collaborate with teachers and principals to make the cafeteria a better place for kids and wants to build lasting relationships with students and their families. Toni even helped to create a weekly club for our students, teaching them about healthy food, how to grow plants, and how to live a happy, healthy life. Her passion for helping our kids inspires everyone to utilize their talents for the betterment of our school.

2. Brave

All progress begins with someone who is brave. When we think of someone who is brave, we often imagine a warrior geared in steel, powerful and unafraid. But being brave does not mean you are not scared. Bravery often means you are trembling and terrified, but you step into the fight anyway. You do the right thing, no matter the risk. You confront the unknown with hope in your heart.

I currently work with one of the bravest individuals I have ever known, Ashley O'Daniel, a social worker in our building. She has a huge heart and is always willing to do whatever it takes to support kids and adults. Ashley is considerate, but she will say what needs to be said for change to occur even when it means having a difficult conversation. She pairs her bravery with her best intentions and always keeps her sights set on the brightest future for our students. Ashley embraces and loves diversity of thought, people, and ideologies. She initiated our school's Social Justice Student Team with two other outstanding educators and a group of students. This team has helped students feel heard, appreciated, and empowered. What I love most about Ashley is that she is always willing to have the courageous conversations to help us all be better people. We all need an Ashley in our schools.

3. Vulnerable

Love and vulnerability are the only bridges that can unite us. When people express an unpopular belief, try something new, ask for help, and admit that they made a mistake, they are vulnerable. Being open and vulnerable allows you to be seen, but sometimes that exposure can be enough to scare us away.

Ironically enough, when you are around vulnerable people, you naturally become more vulnerable. Seeing others share often gives you permission to do the same. People who "dare greatly," as author Brené Brown puts it, can be the catalyst to help themselves and others be all they can be.

4. Accepting of Others

When we think of the idea of accepting others, there is more to it than we would like to admit. Accepting others is not . . .

- Making sure others do things that make you happy
- Directing others to be more like you
- Having people do things your way

Accepting others for who they are is a lifelong skill that we must practice daily. Accepting others gives them permission to be everything they are.

PEOPLE ARE MORE LIKELY TO GROW AND BE THE BEST VERSIONS OF THEMSELVES WHEN THEY ARE CONNECTED WITH THOSE WHO ACCEPT THEM FOR WHO THEY ARE.

---

5. Tenacious

What are you tenacious about? Is your tenacity displayed in how you put your T3—passions, skills, and personality traits—into action?

Those who are tenacious are persistent and exude determination. They might be tempted to give up, but they don't. These individuals do take a moment to breathe and regain their vision, but they always keep their eye turned to the future.

The Bottom Line

The process of building meaningful relationships cannot be forced. A relationship is built on love, trust, and authenticity. We need to take just as much time building relationships with our staff as we do with our students. How we treat each other as adults will flow downstream to our students. For this reason and many others, we can live a fuller and deeper life if we see our colleagues as more than people we see at work. These people can be more than co-workers; they can be our family.

Some of my most meaningful bonds have been forged at work with colleagues. We take care of and inspire one another by knowing our hearts and lifting one another up to keep doing what we do. We need one another.

I encourage everyone reading this to hug a co-worker, say thank you, be a family, and show your love.

JOURNAL

What traits would you add to the list of "traits of people who inspire others"?

_____

_____

_____

_____

Who inspires you to be all you are?

_____

_____

_____

_____

What do they do that inspires you?

_____

_____

_____

_____

What are your biggest barriers to being present in the moment?

_____

_____

_____

_____

_____

_____

What steps can you take to be conscious and focused on the now?

_____

_____

_____

_____

_____

_____

DISCUSSION QUESTIONS

- Does every staff member in your building greet students? If not, how can you help build a culture where everyone is welcoming to one another and to visitors?

- It is easy to get along with people with whom we have a natural connection. What about people who are different from you and with whom you might not see eye to eye? How do you connect with those people? What might you do differently?

- Think of a role model who embodies a servant heart. How do they behave, and how do their actions impact others?

- When you make mistakes at work, how do others treat you? What would you change about that if you could? What kind of response would help you grow?

The human voice is the
most perfect instrument
of all.

Arvo Part

CHAPTER 8

Empower Staff Voice

THROUGHOUT MY EXPERIENCE AS a leader, I have grown and developed my vision and beliefs. I know that without a doubt, I will continue to evolve. To keep growing, I rely heavily on my team for feedback. I always look forward to acquiring new insights and perspectives. Through working closely with other staff members, I have learned so much about what each staff member has to offer our school and the world.

We need their voices shared with others. Our school is not just our personal school—it is *our* school. Sharing our voice helps give us all agency in our community.

Thirteen Questions

To empower staff voice, employees must have the opportunity to offer input and ask questions. Leaders are fond of saying, "My door is always open," but we need to prop open that door and invite people inside. They need to know they have permission to speak freely. This requires school leaders to move beyond simply being present. We need to ask more thoughtful questions that will help us understand the many different roles of our team members. The next step is to genuinely care about the answer. Anyone can ask a question, but the most effective leaders listen and act upon the answers they receive.

Here are thirteen questions aimed at helping you gain more insight into your staff members and your colleagues. Later in the chapter, I will show you how to adapt these same questions for kids to help you better connect with your students. These questions are also a great starting point for self-reflection.

1. What do you love most about your work?
2. What was a highlight that happened at work within the last week?
3. What are your biggest hurdles at work?
4. How can I support you during these hurdles?
5. Is there any feedback you can give me on how I am doing in my role?
6. What am I doing well in?
7. What am I overlooking?
8. How do I need to grow to best meet the needs of our staff and students?
9. What do you feel is the biggest obstacle for our organization as a whole right now?
10. Do we have an elephant in the room?
11. If so, how might we address it?
12. Do you believe you have an opportunity to use your talents at work?
13. How can I help you unleash your talents with students, staff, and the community?

Once you know the answers to these questions, you can better unleash talent in your school by having a better understanding of how you can grow, what your colleagues need, and what environments and conditions they need to succeed; for example, when I am collaborating with staff members on their growth plans for the year, I intentionally embed a few of these questions into our discussions. My favorite questions from the list are . . .

- How can I support you?
- Is there any feedback you can give me on how I am doing in my role?
- How do I need to grow to best meet the needs of our staff and students?

I make sure to listen, resist becoming defensive, and truly take their words to heart. Including my own growth in the conversation helps set a collaborative tone and demonstrates that I believe we can learn from each other.

Be vulnerable, be brave, and start by asking staff members one-on-one a few of these questions and see what happens. Your staff members will appreciate your efforts more than you know. Sometimes during these conversations, I hear groundbreaking wisdom from them that gives me a completely new perspective on an issue. Other times, I learn little things we can incorporate into our school that will have a huge impact on staff.

During one of these conversations with a teacher, I asked the question, "How can I better support you?" She said she and other teachers wanted more opportunities for vertical team planning with their departments. This teacher had recently attended an incredible conference and wanted to share what she had learned with others. I listened, communicated this with the team, and within a few days, we scheduled a planning session on one of our early-release days. As soon as the teacher saw this on the calendar, she emailed me with the biggest thank you.

We might not be able to grant every request we receive, but we need to do everything in our power to try. The effort of following through is noticed by your colleagues. If they believe you care and listen to what they say, they are more likely to continue to share their thoughts with you.

I recently met with one of our incredible secretaries, Brandi Callahan, and asked her, "Is there any feedback you can give me on how I am doing in my role?" She told me I could do a better job of utilizing her and delegating work. Brandi mentioned that she could see all of the enormous tasks on my plate and had offered to help ease the burden, but I had declined the help. So I asked her what she believed her strengths were and how I could better use those strengths when my plate became crowded. Brandi told me the projects she was interested in taking on and the tasks she wanted to help me manage. Our conversation helped me realize that by not adding to her workload, I was making her feel that I did not want or need her help. Her honest feedback was a wake-up call, reminding me that relying on others can also help them feel valued. By turning to Brandi for help in specific areas, I can also unleash her specific talents.

Brandi now creates incredible spreadsheets that I could never create myself and solves problems that I didn't even know existed. I call her Nancy Drew because she has an eye for hidden details and patterns that most people miss. She corrects me when I make mistakes, helps me grow, and sees problems before they happen.

If I hadn't asked her how I could improve in my role or taken action based on what she said, I would have never realized the full extent of her talents or what I could improve upon. We all bring useful talents and perspectives to the table, and when we bring those out into the open, our schools will be better for it.

To empower staff voice, we need to help each other understand the following:

- We value different perspectives
- We need your voice and will subsequently listen to your voice
- Your voice can and should be used to make a positive impact

Thirteen Questions for Students

As promised, here are thirteen questions for teachers to ask their students. Before asking these questions, keep in mind that you will not want to necessarily ask all the questions at once, and you will want to be purposeful about the questions you do ask. You might want to provide more context and explain what you mean by the questions. Some questions might need to be adjusted or expanded upon based on the level of students you teach. When I was a teacher, I asked my students many of these questions throughout the year to learn more about them and to then adjust my teaching to their needs. I also loved asking my students how I could become better as an educator. Who better to give you feedback on your teaching skills than the students in your classes?

1. What do you love most about school?

2. What do you love most about our class?

3. What do you like to learn about?

4. Think of a learning moment, lesson, or activity that we did during class that you enjoyed. What was the activity, and why did you enjoy it?

5. What makes you curious?

6. What is your favorite thing that happened at school this week?

7. What are some tough things that you experience at school?

8. How can I help you during those tough times?

9. What can I do better as a teacher to help you learn?

10. What do you love to do for fun at home?

11. What are your biggest strengths as a learner?

12. Name some of your talents in and out of school. Do you have the chance to show your strengths and talents at school?

13. How can I give more chances for you to show your strengths and talents in our class?

Our students have more talents, strengths, interests, and curiosity inside of them than we can ever imagine or understand. It's our responsibility to give our students opportunities to share their thoughts and ask questions. When we shift to meet our students' needs, we are helping them become who they are meant to be.

A Caveat to Working with the Same People

We are all different and that's beautiful.

— **Karen Salmansohn**

When we plan with groups of people, we tend to gravitate toward those with whom we are most comfortable. When we are up against a deadline, we tend to rely on our closest allies for advice. When working with the same people and teams over time, this is a natural occurrence. We do not mean to be magnets to some people and alienate others, but it can happen.

As a teacher, I initially gravitated toward people who were similar to me. Over time, through experience, I learned to appreciate the differences of others rather than running from them. I began to lean into the people who were my polar opposites, learning from their gifts without fear and judgment.

I remember working with a teacher who I thought disliked me. She always seemed to shy away from conversation with me and questioned my ideas. It turns out, she didn't dislike me at all; in fact, she was quite fond of me. The issue was really the way we communicated. I'm an extrovert who approaches everything with enthusiasm. She's an introvert who likes to analyze and be 100 percent sure before trying something new. I didn't figure that out until someone else explained her thought process to me.

It's also important to have variety among departments, grade-level partners, and teams. It's great to work with people who have similar talents, but if all teachers on a team are super extroverted and theatrical, they might only come up with lessons and activities based around those traits.

To better communicate with people who might be different from you, keep these points in mind:

Welcome New Mindsets

Remember throughout your daily grind that life is best lived outside your comfort zone. It keeps you fresh, diverse, and connected to the whole team not just your team. You will often need to defend or explain your viewpoint, which reminds you of why you have it in the first place while further pushing your thinking.

Earlier this school year, a few teachers approached our administrative team, wanting ideas to help with challenging student behaviors in a way that would help students think more critically about their habits while also helping them adapt their behaviors in more positive ways. I suggested a toolbox of strategies and philosophy called "Love and Logic" (LoveandLogic.com/teaching-with-love-and-logic) that has been useful to me as an educator and as a leader. In short, Love and Logic gives practical tools that can be used to help build positive student and teacher relationships, de-escalate student behavior, and make teaching and learning more fun as a result.

At first, a few teachers expressed apprehension about the idea, and rightfully so. It is healthy, natural, and necessary to push back and constructively challenge ideas. I asked these teachers to give me a chance to show them the strategies, and if they did not like them, we would find another approach together. They agreed and were willing to give it a try; therefore, I started by attending one of their team meetings. During this time, I shared with them how these strategies had provided effective ways to support students when they were dysregulated and to also help students gain more voice and choice. I also shared helpful tips and meaningful language that teachers could implement in their classroom that same day.

I was ecstatic when, before we even left the first session, they asked when our next learning session would be so they could book it on their calendars!

As we continued to dive into learning, these incredible teachers had the idea of starting their own book study on Love and Logic. Through their excitement during this process, they shared the positive strides their new approach had helped them make in their classrooms and in their own way of thinking. These teachers have now been partnering together to create and lead school-wide professional development based on their learning.

Watching these teachers embrace new knowledge while making it their own has truly touched my heart. Even when moments were difficult, they have been willing to push through and to strive to find another way to help our kids.

Understand Different Personality Types

As I mentioned in earlier in the book, understanding your personality type and the personality types of others can be crucial to unleashing talent. Without that understanding, it's easier to be personally offended by someone's actions and communication style; for example, some personality types might want you to provide examples when explaining their thought process, while other personality types would prefer for you to show the big picture.

My former colleagues, lifelong friends, and one of the best teacher teams I have ever worked with, show how they began their journey as a new team and learned more about one another and their personality types to become strong collaborators and friends. I have seen that through their collaboration and through lifting one another up, they have been even stronger for the students they serve. Fourth- and fifth-grade teachers in Independence, Missouri—Angie, Molly, and Lauren—share their story here:

We don't think any of us realized how well we would work together in the beginning, but we were all excited and knew we had been hired for a common mission and purpose. We bought into the goals and direction of our school, and that, we believe, was certainly a driving force that brought us to where we are today. Molly and Angie had been teaching for years (too many to count), and Lauren was relatively new to the profession. Regardless, our ages and years of experience didn't seem to cause any differences. We quickly discovered that we had similar philosophies on education and how to love on kids and do great work.

Each of us inherently figured out one another's strengths and where we could contribute for the good of the group. An activity that we did as a staff well before school started was discovering what personality type we had based on compass points: North, South, East, and West. When it was time for staff members to move to their respective compass points, the three of us split up. We ended up at North, South, and East. One would think that this would cause problems or issues between the three of us, but it only seemed to solidify why we could work so well together and why we get so much accomplished.

It all seems to boil down to respect. Because we have sought out the gifts and talents in one another, we are able to respect one another professionally and personally. We support one another; we care about one another's lives and well-being both inside and outside the classroom. This allows us to be bonded and successful as a team. Not a planning time goes by that we aren't together figuring things out, facing the tough stuff together, and driving one another to be the best versions of ourselves. The great part about all of that is, we are never in it alone. We always have each other to help figure things out and make our work the best it can be. We may not always agree, but our respect for one another maintains it all in the end.

Feedback, Feedback, Feedback

In an article on SoapBoxHQ.com, blogger Bryan Rusche cited a study on feedback in the workplace stating, "According to a survey conducted by leadership trainers, Zenger Folkman looked into the feedback practices of twenty-two thousand leaders around the world and found that leaders who scored in the top 10 percent on giving feedback had employees who were three times more engaged than employees with leaders scoring in the bottom 10 percent. The study also revealed that the bottom 10 percent of leaders had employees who were three times more likely to think about quitting."

Teachers and administration leaders alike can both take part in these strategies to empower voice in one another:

- Be an unofficial coach
- Ask insightful questions

Find time to meet with people individually. Feedback can be a word with far and wide negative connotation. When others ask for our feedback, we wonder sometimes, "Do you want to know the whole story of what I really think; or just the good or bad parts?"

It can be absolutely terrifying to share what we really think. When offering feedback, it is important to understand the other person's personality; for example, if the person is more conservative and needs to do research before feeling comfortable moving forward, try providing articles that support your points when giving them feedback.

In general, when soliciting and giving feedback, you want to be mindful of the following:

HOW YOU ASK FOR FEEDBACK

Are you asking for feedback in ways that seem genuine, authentic, and full of good intention? Do you always ask for feedback through e-mail or surveys, or do you embed personal and one-on-one time when seeking feedback?

HOW YOU VALUE IT

Are you asking because you want to hear what others think or because you feel like you have to ask? People can usually sniff this out.

HOW YOU MOVE FORWARD WITH IT

It is impossible to take in every single person's feedback and change everything all at once. Some try this and fail. If you take this approach, you will be doomed to a stressful and fatigued work environment. Sometimes it is necessary to make a change that is against the norm. Trust your gut and give yourself permission to take risks.

Questions to Consider When Reviewing and Taking in Feedback

- Do you need to make a plan as a result of the feedback? If so, what should the plan entail to be successful?
- What thoughts and considerations were embedded when developing the plan?
- Who else did you team up with to put the plan together?
- What can others do to help and make this plan a success?
- How will you regularly monitor and receive feedback once the plan is up and running?
- When will you know things are not working? When will you know when pieces of the plan need to change? When will you know when to celebrate what is working?

Important mention: When I say "plan" above, I mean anything you and your team are doing at your school to grow or change. This encompasses many areas: creating a new curricular unit, developing a safety or crisis plan in your building, establishing a school-wide mission and vision, monitoring PLCs, and more.

Know Your Audience

We are in a world that relies on digital surveys and forms to collect our opinions.

While this can be seamless, fast, and handy, too many surveys and forms lead to broken relationships. Surveys are a good way to compile initial data for discussion, but it is not the space for discussion to take place. Technology will never replace us. We still need opportunities to talk with one another one-on-one and to have heart-to-hearts that feel warm and non-confrontational. Without our screens, we are able to read body language, to hear voice intonation patterns, and to be better prepared to address needs as they arise.

But despite what method you are implementing to talk to others, know your audience. Whether you are a teacher looking for more curricular ideas to embed in the classroom or a superintendent wanting to gain feedback on a recent program, think about your audience and how you can use each opportunity to gain the biggest bang for your buck, not just in information gained but in improved interpersonal relationships too.

Building relationships should be a part of everything we do, not a separate entity. Do not get me wrong. Surveys and forms can be great ways to accumulate pieces of information during the right times, but they should never be the end-all-be-all.

The Quietest Voices

When discussing feedback, we have to do a better job of not just accepting feedback from our most outgoing teachers but from our quietest teachers too. Even the quietest teacher voices have an opinion, and we have to help those teachers find ways to share their voice and bring it to the table.

In one of my favorite books of all time, *Lean In: Women, Work, and the Will to Lead,* author and Facebook CEO Sheryl Sandberg says, "We hold ourselves back in ways both big and small by lacking self-confidence, by not raising our hands, and by pulling back when we should be leaning in." Sometimes people are quiet in sharing their thoughts because they are introverts. We should be careful not to assume that they lack confidence or have little to offer. In reality, people who are quiet and more reserved are often exceptional listeners and problem solvers.

While growing up with two brothers and a dad who were introverted, I learned how to adapt my extroverted personality to different environments so that it was not overbearing. Here are some points I learned from personal and career experience:

- During professional development, team, or department meetings, teachers, nurses, secretaries, administrators, custodians, central office members, and others should find ways to build time for personal reflection outside of the group. We often focus all professional development on collaboration but minimize the importance of reflection and time with oneself to become one with our ideas.
- Create a balance between group and independent time during professional development, learning opportunities, and throughout the school day.
- Teacher blog: We often encourage students to blog and share their ideas but face a disconnect when it comes to the number of teachers who also blog. Encourage your staff to blog and share their thoughts. Writing, blogging, and sharing blogs with other staff members is a great way to empower the quietest voices.
- Sleep On It: Pose a question, idea, or thought to staff and have them sleep on it and think on it for a night or more. Introverts often think deeply about an idea and need time to process before sharing with others.
- Last but not least, remember many of these same ideas for staff are applicable for students as well.

Share Your Voice

Raise your words, not your voice. It is rain that grows flowers, not thunder.

—**RUMI**

Do not wait for staff meetings or professional development opportunities to empower others to share their voices. Look or create opportunities on the edges to meet people where they are emotionally throughout the school day or at another scheduled time.

Keep in mind, these opportunities do not always need to be growth focused. As a former classroom teacher, I did team-building and class-building exercises weekly, but I didn't always base them around content. Once a week, we did a team-building exercise that had nothing to do with content. To illustrate, I always had the book *Silly Sports and Goofy Games* by Spencer Kagan on my desk for quick and easy reference. I tabbed, highlighted, and folded page corners to mark my favorite silly sports or goofy games. I heartily recommend this book for every teacher in all grade levels. Within this book, you will find fun team-building games spelled out step by step. I have also used many of these same activities for staff too.

Get to know your colleagues as people as well as educators, just as we should know our students. When we build those relationships and we can ask about our colleagues' families by name, it's a lot easier and safer to give feedback.

No matter who we are, if we are waiting until a staff meeting to share our feedback or to request it from others, we most likely have a broken system. Feedback does not need a meeting place. It needs a vulnerable space and someone to truly listen.

My Challenge to You

I urge you to try one of these fun activities to get to know your colleagues inside and outside of the classroom:

- Ask a colleague whom you do not know well to eat in your classroom/office with you at lunch or to meet somewhere for dinner. Getting to know a colleague more can help you gather information about their comfort level so that they can share their voice with you, and vice versa.
- Host a Coffee edu (coffeeedu.org) gathering before school, after school, or on the weekend to meet with your colleagues and even other educators within your city to share voices in an informal and unconference-like environment. Coffee and conversation always go hand-in-hand. If you do not like coffee, host an ice cream social or an appetizer gathering.
- Think outside the box to include as many people as possible: Last year, each grade-level team at my school was in charge of creating a fun gathering for staff during their chosen month. During our gathering days, we held Breakout Box activities, dinners, bowling nights, barbecues, and more.

The Bottom Line

If you want to win in the 21st century, you have to empower others, making sure other people are better than you are.
Then you will be successful.

—**JACK MA**

To empower staff voice, we must build relationships with our staff members, understand our role in helping others share their voice and talents, and respect the personality, background, and cultural differences of others.

Our unique voice to share with others is a representation of our T3—our passions, skills, and personality traits. How we share that voice is a direct correlation to how we share our gift with others and how we also help others feel comfortable sharing their gift with us.

As fashion designer Diane von Furstenberg says, "I have always believed that when you have a voice, you have an obligation to share that voice with others." Only you can share your unique story with colleagues, family, friends, and the world. Use your voice to inspire and uplift your school community and the world around you for the better.

JOURNAL

What other ideas do you have for promoting staff voice at your school?

_____

_____

_____

_____

_____

_____

_____

How can you help others contribute their ideas at staff gatherings and activities?

_____

_____

_____

_____

_____

_____

DISCUSSION QUESTIONS

- Do you ask colleagues for feedback on the work that you do? How can you shift the way you ask for feedback to grow further in your practice?

- How do you recognize different personality types in your building and find ways to communicate better rather than fall into traps of isolation?

- How can you find ways to empower the quietest voices in your building? How could you help these people share their perspectives and talents?

- What are some other opportunities on the edges that you can find or create to learn more about your colleagues?

PART 4

Understanding Talent and Its Impact

Coming together is a beginning. Keeping together is progress. Working together is success.

———

Henry Ford

CHAPTER 9

Talent to Transform Schools

MANY PEOPLE LOOK TO technology to transform schools, and it must play a part. Cutting-edge digital tools and platforms are evolving rapidly and providing educators with amazing opportunities, but technology alone cannot get the job done. We spend countless dollars on the latest tools and gadgets when we should be investing in our greatest resource: our people. Unleashing the talent of that human capital—the teachers, media specialists, cafeteria workers, school nurses, principals, tutors, bus drivers—is the key to transforming entire school communities and producing students who are truly equipped for the future that awaits. In cultivating their T3, their passions, skills, and personality traits, we are encouraging a generation of teachers to be their authentic selves. When we unleash the talents of our teachers and other adults, we ultimately unleash the talents of our students.

WHEN WE UNLEASH THE TALENTS OF OUR TEACHERS AND OTHER ADULTS, WE ULTIMATELY UNLEASH THE TALENTS OF OUR STUDENTS.

Bringing Out the Color

We all have different gifts,
so we all have different ways of
saying to the world who we are.

—**FRED ROGERS**

In the short film *Alike*, a father and his son live in a society where the workload and rigidness of conformity literally take the color from them. Their color can only be regained by finding the creativity and happiness within them. In the film, you see the father continually losing his color, partially due to the overload of menial tasks given to him that seem to take away his happiness, creativity, and purpose. He clocks in, does his work, clocks out when his shift is over, goes home, and feels too drained to do anything else. The next day, he wakes up and does it all over again. Day after day, he works without ever getting ahead or experiencing any satisfaction. Without realizing it, he passes down his sadness to his son. This film has such a serious parallel to real life.

At most schools, we are asking our staff members to take on more and more responsibilities, sometimes to their detriment. We force them to spend time on activities and tasks that are not making a positive difference in the lives of students, and in a sense, we are partially to blame for our tired, overworked society. More importantly, adults who are drained and hopeless will pass on those same feelings to their students. When we are filled with color, we fill up others with color. When we lose our color, we drain those around us. Whether or not we are trying, our feelings, our energy, and our hopes will always affect other people

To truly transform our schools, we must create environments where diving into your T3, your passions, skills, personality traits, is the norm, not the exception. This mindset should be our starting point, not just some idea we squeeze into our schedule if we find the time. What if we replaced those ineffective activities with learning opportunities that brought forth a student's or teacher's individual color? What if we decided to stimulate the color of staff and students at the same time? What might that look like?

To help shed light on how I have pushed forward in bringing more color into where I reside, I will share one of my favorite experiences and stories of bringing color into our schools:

As many of us know, Edcamps (edcamp.org) for teachers have taken the educational world by storm. Teachers, including myself, have been refreshed and renewed with the Edcamp style of learning, which consists of learning and sharing in an unconference format. My favorite part of Edcamps is that the attendee organically determines what they want to learn that day based on their passions, questions, wonderings, and journey of learning. Edcamps are a perfect way to build upon your T3 without even realizing it.

After being a part of many Edcamps across the nation, attending an Edcamp Leadership Summit, and creating and co-leading a city-wide Edcamp, I felt a stirring in my heart to also try it with students. I thought, *If we know Edcamps are beneficial for adults, isn't worth a try to allow students to experience them as well?*

Therefore, based on my wonderings last year, I worked with colleagues to create Edcamps for students (bit.ly/kkstudentedcamps). Within our Student Edcamp process, students and teachers were able to vote on and create sessions that they wanted to be a part of. As we decided which rooms in which to house the learning and sessions, teachers chose to also supervise the rooms that housed the sessions and topics that they were most passionate about.

My favorite part about the format was seeing our students and staff sitting in a big circle on the ground, listening and collaborating with one another. By the end of the Edcamp, I was able to learn so much about the strengths that our students and staff members possessed that I never knew before. To illustrate, during one of the Edcamp days, students wanted to lead a soccer discussion on how the game of soccer works. They wanted an opportunity to share their most epic experiences as soccer players while talking about the skill set of the sport. But during the session, one student said, "Hey, let's stop talking about soccer, and let's actually play it!" So we quickly borrowed a soccer ball from our P.E. teacher and played a game in the small but quaint cafeteria space that we had.

In another classroom, students and teachers were teaching each other how to code while sharing tricks of the trade. In another space, students began connecting, sharing, and discussing their love for rocks: fun facts they knew about rocks, rock cycles, and rock formations. In another session, I was even able to spontaneously show students how to use apps to digitally create and enhance video clips.

Through interacting with students and teachers during these sessions and observing their conversations, I was able to learn more about their personal lives, talents, and passions that I never previously saw in that capacity or fullness. In addition, students who once believed they did not have anything in common with unlikely classmates found common interests that built friendships that might not have happened without the Edcamp. These student Edcamps have become some of the favorite moments of my career thus far. Not only were we able to see students and teachers showing color in their lives, but we saw their T3 come forward full-circle. Nothing beats real opportunities for learning where students and adults are able to showcase their talents, skills, and personality traits. (Learn more about how we did our Edcamp by scanning this QR code:

Feel free to mold, adapt, and completely change what we did to fit your students and staff.)

I have found that it is not enough to just ask students and teachers what they are passionate about at the beginning of the year; we must give them a chance to *live* their passion during the school day, passions that might not be academic. We must allow them to broaden their potential to grow into who they are and who they want to be rather than what school wants them to be. When you see people at their happiest, doing what they are passionate about, you will never forget it. You will never see that person the same way, and you will begin to remember them for the gifts they have to share and what they have to offer rather than what they might lack.

Throughout my time as an educator, I have learned that not one program or event can be a Holy Grail for transformation in your school. I have been willing to try anything and everything in order to see how I can unleash the talent in my staff, my students, and myself. This willingness to try new things has been an important piece of unleashing talent. In the past, my students have created podcasts, developed a Makerspace, and collaborated to develop flexible learning spaces. My students and staff members have written, created and participated in blogs. My students have created self-driven playlists to lead their own innovative learning, and my staff members have led their own learning and professional development by earning badges. All of these opportunities have been magnificent points of growth and learning. Through each occasion, you find out what works for your students and staff, what does not, and how to expand it to make it even better for all. These experiences allowed for many of us to see one another in different lights while providing ways to unleash talent in us all.

**Student
Podcast**

**Makerspace &
Flexible Learning
Spaces**

**Self-Driven
Playlists**

But having said that, not one Edcamp or Makerspace will be the key to transformation. Using these experiences as a fix-all will only act as a temporary bandage to underlying problems. But if these opportunities are done with meaning and with true collaboration between staff members and students where everyone can share their T3, we can uplift our community and bring life and color to the spaces we occupy.

Multiple Chances for Success

There is no glory in practice, but without practice, there is no glory.

—**UNKNOWN**

Unleashing talent is not about putting on an event or talent show that only happens once a year. Unleashing talent happens as a result of many people purposefully providing multiple, continuous, and varied opportunities to their community over time in order to showcase its passions, skills, and personality traits. It is similar to building a relationship with another person; it does not happen overnight, and it takes time grow and flourish. Your first idea might not be a home run, but it might lead to your second and third ideas, and those might lead to even more ways to showcase the talent in your school community. Don't give up—maintain your momentum! Give yourself and others multiple chances for success, or as some call it, targeted practice. In *The Talent Code,* author Daniel Coyle describes the complexity of practice in this way: "Deep practice is built on a paradox: Struggling in certain targeted ways—operating at the edges of your ability, where you make mistakes—makes you smarter. Or to put it a slightly different way, experiences where you're forced to slow down, make errors, and correct them—as you would if you were walking up an ice-covered hill, slipping and stumbling as you go—end up making you swift and graceful without your realizing it."

I love this idea that pushing through a struggle and discomfort is necessary to growth. Temporary discomfort is proof that you are making progress. If you want to move closer to your talents and further away from your doubts, you must embrace discomfort, seeking it out instead of running away from it. But keep in mind that the discomfort is really just a catalyst. The defining moment comes when we respond to the discomfort. We can give up and walk away, or we can slow down, correct course, and keep going. The latter, I believe, is the only way to truly develop talent.

During my freshman year of high school, I started running track. I had this idea that I would love running and that I would especially love running sprints. I envisioned myself gliding gracefully across the terra-cotta-colored track curve, smiling without a care in the world. Needless to say, my perception versus the reality were two very different things. After a few weeks of serious practice, running nonstop in the heat and pushing myself beyond my physical limits, I was ready to call it quits. As a somewhat dramatic fifteen-year-old, I declared to my parents, "I absolutely hate running and never want to do it ever, ever again!" Given my parents' moral code and their belief in never giving up, I should have foreseen how this conversation would end. I tried to find some wiggle room, but there was none. My parents informed me that I would finish the track season, and then I could decide if I wanted to continue the following year. Upon hearing this, of course, I labeled them "the worst parents in the world" and couldn't believe they would require me to participate in a sport I completely hated. Looking back, however, it was the best thing they could have done for me at that moment.

On that track, I learned to reject the easy choice, push through the discomfort, and overcome obstacles in my path; furthermore, I found out that running was not so terrible. To this day, while I don't always enjoy running, and I know I am not the fastest runner, I love how I feel afterward. I sometimes run when my mind is racing, when I need a little me time, or when I want to feel the success of running a couple of miles. If my parents had not stood firm all those years ago in their expectations of me, I might have never discovered my passion for running. It goes to show that everyday decisions, people, and influences make huge contributions to developing a person's T3.

Spoon Feeding or Empowering?

Although we have good intentions with the learning experiences we provide to students and staff members, we can become stuck in a pattern of doing what we've always done. Worse yet, we can also force-feed knowledge to people rather than giving others the opportunity to learn for themselves. These ruts and sequences of behavior actually suppress the passion we are trying to encourage in one another; nevertheless, I believe we are capable of rewiring our thinking to foster and inspire new ideas, new passions, new interests, and new talents.

Imagine how school could be transformed if more learning was voluntary, ongoing, and if staff and students were self-motivated and empowered to learn; for example . . .

- Are students and adults given the power to decide to an extent how they will learn each day?
- Are only adults leading the learning in your classroom or building, or are students also given this same opportunity?

Based on your answers to the bulleted questions above, make small tweaks to your day-by-day approach to include these elements and watch the progress that occurs. While you organize your day, create your content and curriculum, and interact with others, keep these questions at the center of what you and your school does. Every single person in every single role has an opportunity to be a part of this process. Practice does not make perfect, but ongoing practice will transform learning and breed talent.

The Little Things Matter

We can grow talent in both small and big ways, and both choices are important. Dwight Carter, principal in New Albany, Ohio, believes in transforming schools by starting small. Dwight shares his story here:

One key factor in being an educator is the ability to use one's personal talents, gifts, or interests to transform one's classroom or school. When

I began teaching twenty-four years ago, I enjoyed doing bulletin boards because empty bulletin boards indicated that we didn't care about the students or learning environment. To me, it was like an abandoned lot or home.

I have the ability to draw (somewhat), so I drew a caricature of myself on a bulletin board just inside my classroom door and titled it, "Carter's Kids." This is where I would highlight the names of my Students of the Month. The personal touch of the caricature and name resonated with students so they worked hard to earn this recognition. Later in the school year, we experienced a series of fights at school that were disruptive to our school climate, increased tension, and hurt the overall morale. Since I spent a majority of my time at school, I decided to use art to send a message about unity.

In the main hallway was a long bulletin board that hadn't been updated since the first day of school. Again, it sent a negative message because no one took the time to change it. The edges were torn, the border was hanging off, and it just looked unkempt. It was directly across from the cafeteria, so every student could see it throughout the day as they ate lunch.

I used white chalk on a black paper to draw Earth: on one side of Earth, I colored the land white, and on the other side, I colored the water white. I then drew two hands holding up the globe: one I colored white, and the other I left black. I included a quote about unity and covered the board with a thin layer of plastic to protect the chalk.

The next day at school, the principal, teachers, and students were in awe of the board. My principal asked why I did it, and I said something about how I wanted to help bring the school together. He was appreciative of what I had done and so were my colleagues. The board and quote was used as inspiration to talk with students about unity during homeroom or study hall. We didn't experience another fight at school that year.

Change starts with small moves forward. Shifts can begin with a purposeful change to a bulletin board that builds excitement by showcasing the positive within a school as in the example above. Joy can begin with a custodian who leaves kind notes on your desk to lift your day, as I have experienced in the past. Gratitude can be shown by praising the efforts that your guidance school secretary makes in order to make every single individual feel that they are welcome in their building. The little things matter. Every single person and their small efforts matter. When we showcase talent, we showcase our appreciation for the person as well. How we embrace those efforts can be the building blocks of how talent is formed at our schools over time. When we showcase talent, others will showcase talent, and the cycle will continually grow.

Unleash!

All it takes is one person, one idea, and a sense of bravery to share this idea with others to catapult transformation in school in which others feel empowered to follow suit. Once we are able to do this as staff, this same way of thinking in how we approach our students can trickle down to them, which is the ultimate goal.

THIS IS WHAT WE SHOULD AIM FOR: NOT TO BE THE SOLE IDEA MACHINE OURSELVES BUT TO CREATE ENVIRONMENTS WHERE STUDENTS AND STAFF CAN LEAD, SHOWCASE THEIR TALENTS, AND TRULY SHINE.

When I see students in our building who are comfortable enough to go to teachers and administration with ideas that they have about how to make the school better, it lifts my heart to new dimensions. When I see students leading and showcasing their talents without fear of what others might think, I feel fulfilled as an observer. This is what we should aim for: not to be the sole idea machine ourselves but to create environments where students and staff can lead, showcase their talents, and truly shine. It is not enough to help our students lead for the future; we need to help them lead now. We are so focused on preparing them for the future that we do not prepare them for today.

When I think of all the talents of various colleagues I have worked with, past and present, it takes my breath away to think of all the incredible deeds they have done to make all of us and the school a better place, sometimes without even realizing it. I think of the times when colleagues blew us away with their skill sets, and we did not even know they had this talent before that moment. Everyone has talents, but sometimes people need someone to push them to unleash it in an environment where they feel comfortable in doing so. The same is probably occurring in your school.

When I reflect upon this school year, I think of . . .

- Teachers who planned a Rap Battle across curriculum, in which students *and* teachers created their own raps that featured what they were learning in the classroom. On the day of the final presentation, I had the honor of seeing students and teachers sitting and standing in a circle, watching their colleagues and teachers performing their final rap. Hearing the cheers, listening to their brilliant raps, adding my fair share of applause, and seeing the excitement in the eyes of students and teachers showed me that talent was bursting at the seams around me.
- Students who bravely led assemblies based on personal passions, such as exercise and public speaking, to help spread fitness and nutrition awareness to their classmates.

- Students who placed notes of kindness during their lunch break on every single locker in their grade-level hallway with uplifting praise, such as, "You are valued. You matter here. You are important." These notes made the day of so many students and continued to inspire acts of kindness during the weeks that followed.
- Students who have created after-school groups based on their passions and skills. These groups allowed the school-wide formation of new connections and friendships.
- Staff members who voluntarily began a school-wide donation drive to collect money for hurricane victims across the country.
- Custodians who work diligently during every school event to make sure we have enough chairs for every family member, every staff member, and every student who attends. The number of hours they devote to each event never ceases to impress me.
- A teacher who worked with her students to create presentations in a setting similar to *Shark Tank*. Students used their knowledge of math, business, money, and investments to create a product and produce a pitch for the product to a real audience.

Identity Day

Each of the above examples displayed talent. Talent can be shown in the way in which people care for others, think creatively, innovate, embrace their passion, use their skill sets to better themselves and others, and use the talents of others to improve themselves. Talent is all around us. Examples of talent are flowing wildly in my school, and I guarantee you that they are all around in yours as well. We just have to have the right eyes to see and find them.

Another way schools have embraced talent and the uniqueness of others is by hosting an Identity Day within their buildings. Identity Day is dedicated to giving teachers and students a chance to share their interests. Participants create a project about themselves with no criteria or specific parameters. In addition, there is no grade at the end. Not only do staff members get a chance to learn more about their students, but students learn more about one another and their teachers. When we know more about the interests and passions of others, we can better meet them where they are and provide more opportunities for others to show who they are and what makes them happy. Many schools even invite parents to observe or even participate in their own Identity Day projects to spread the love and to embrace talent.

When we create a culture where both staff and students feel that their talents are appreciated and that they can make a change, they will make that change.

Once we have built a bond with many of our staff members in different roles, we must push one another to use our talents for the greater good. Great leaders do not care about showcasing their talents to the entire school. The best leaders use talents to help their staff and students realize how great they are.

Permission to Move Slowly

There is no great achievement that is not the result of patient working and waiting.

—J.G. HOLLAND

Patience is one of the hardest skills to master in life. As Martin Luther King, Jr. once said, "You don't have to see the whole staircase, just take the first step." Those who have patience as one of their T3 skills are truly gifted because, for many of us, patience is a rare virtue. We want change for ourselves, our schools, and our families, and we want it now!

But we aren't especially skilled at playing the long game. The pattern I currently see in education includes going all-in for a short period of time, burning out, losing momentum, and eventually dropping the initiative altogether. Thanks primarily to technological strides, the field of education is moving faster than ever before, and many educators find themselves focusing more on speed than on purpose and collaboration. If we continue in this manner, we're only moving forward for the sake of moving forward, not doing so with meaning.

While reading this book, you might be tempted to put it down and charge full-speed ahead with implementing some of my ideas in your life and at work. If this is your natural inclination, I applaud you, but I also urge you to consider taking the long way around. Summon your patience—I promise it's in there—and settle in for a slower ride. What's the point, you might ask? The best answer I can give you is that although passionate and energetic educators are tremendous assets in any school community, no amount of determination can unleash talent before it's ready to be unleashed. I have seen the most passionate and best-intentioned educators, who wanted nothing more than to innovate, unintentionally bulldoze over others who were not ready. While embracing your talent and the talent of others, be mindful that timing and approach is everything. Gauge the feelings and pulse of those around you when unleashing talent. Some students and colleagues might be ready to push themselves further in their talents personally and professionally while others might be apprehensive, and that is okay.

Confucius once said, "It does not matter how slowly you go as long as you do not stop." Part of unleashing talent is the ability to read those around you and know how hard and when to push. Becoming a caretaker of talent is an art, and it takes plenty of practice. Being a caretaker of talent also can become its own talent if you invest enough time into developing the skill. Above all, remember that when you push others and yourself closer to developing seen or unseen talents, there will be moments of discomfort, and progress might feel excruciatingly slow. Stay persistent and help others and yourself find comfort in the discomfort.

Limit the Barriers

Most of the barriers that we face personally and in schools are created within our own minds. We become the barrier, letting ourselves believe we cannot transform schools because we do not have enough money or resources. These feelings can make us feel helpless. In my career, I have had the experience of working at schools in low-income areas and schools in areas with medium to high incomes. Sadly, people in all kinds of schools use a lack of funding and other resources as an excuse to stop moving forward or to not embrace a challenge. What I have found in each case is that the best barrier blocker and the best resources that we have are our people. If we want to unleash talent and transform schools, we must become resourceful and limit the barriers that do exist.

When I was a teacher, I wanted to help bring out the strengths of all the readers in my class. At the beginning of the year, many of my students said they "hated reading" and "were bad readers." While looking deeper, I noticed that many of my middle school readers did not want to read, because the books they could understand had childish covers and childish content. I always spent money on my classroom library, but I knew I could not sustain the financial burden alone. As I considered the low-income community I taught for and wanted to help support, I knew I needed to think creatively to help provide for my students; therefore, I started looking into books with engaging covers for middle schoolers with content that would relate to students who struggled with reading. I found the company Orca Books and wrote a grant that included high interest, low-level readers with age-level appropriate content and interesting book covers that piqued the interest of my students. I sent my grant request in, and to my surprise, my grant was chosen! Gaining full sets of these books helped students who once were apprehensive about reading gain a love for reading and discover book genres that they never knew about before. Students who once ran far away from my library were diving in, book after book, to read! Seeing the love for reading form in the heart of students was everything and more than I could have wished for.

When my colleagues wanted to give their students an experience with an expert that they would never forget, they reached out to the Ford Corporation to see if a mechanical engineer from the truck plant would come to speak to their students about the work they do, and Ford said "*Yes!*" The Ford engineer brought truck parts to the students, discussed his experience in the plant, and answered any and all questions from the students. This experience and expertise not only connected with their science unit but connected students to a face and experience that helped bring the topic to life in a way in which they could understand, love, and enjoy.

In many circumstances, we use a "lack of resources" as our reason to hold us back. While a lack of resources might hold us back, our lack of resourcefulness will be the biggest barrier of all if we let it. We can find an incredible number of people who are willing to help, support, or give to us if we just ask. Many times, I almost did not ask for help or resources due to a fear of hearing no, but those were the times when I surprisingly heard yes! To help limit any barriers you might have in your community, take a look at any of the websites, resources, and ideas below to help unleash creativity and talent in your school. This list is just a starter, so think outside the box and even beyond this list to find ways to transform your school and to start unleashing talent.

- Connect to businesses, companies, and people through social media to gain resources or expertise. Some of the best resources you can gain might not be donated materials but time to talk with you, your staff, and your students. Many authors, local business members, speakers, and experts love opportunities to come to schools or to Skype or Google Hangout to either share their knowledge, their book, or their time with the youth.

- Watch, listen, and lean into experts by tapping into the knowledge on YouTube. Allow your colleagues and students to do the same. School has no boundaries; learning is everywhere.
- Ask family members within your community to come to your school to share their passions, their expertise, and their hobbies with students.
- Go to the nearest thrift store or Goodwill to pick up books, supplies, and anything else that might encourage students to pursue their passions!
- Apply for grants to gain resources to support your students at one or more of the following:
  - ▶ Fund for Teachers (fundforteachers.org) allows you to apply for grants based on your location.
  - ▶ Adopt A Classroom allows people to donate to classrooms in needs.
  - ▶ Donors Choose (donorschoose.org) connects donors with high-needs communities and schools who need classroom materials, technology, resources, and experiences.
  - ▶ Teach.com is where you can apply for grants that may fit the need of your school, classroom, or area of need.

Working Together to Move Students Forward

The true strength of a classroom lies in the collaboration of learners, not in the knowledge of one expert.

—KRISSY VENOSDALE

We all have talent; we are all worthwhile, and our job titles do not dictate everything we have to offer. When we are able to live and model this idea as adults, we send this same message to our students. True collaboration—everyone from central office leaders and principals to coaches and custodians working toward a common goal—is what will transform our schools. When we work in harmony to unleash talent in one another, we are in the optimal position to unleash talent in our students.

We must believe in ourselves but not only in ourselves. When our egos get in the way, we have to remember that it is not about being the best staff member or leader we can be; it is about bringing out the best in one another so that we can be the best for kids. Our schools were not built to showcase the knowledge of only one person. They were built for the purpose of spreading knowledge across entire communities. When a school connects to its larger community, it touches the world. Sometimes it feels like we're a small piece of the puzzle, but everything we do together as a staff matters. What we do can leave a legacy on students for generations to come.

My dear friend and educator, Dana Ariss from Ontario, Canada, shares a story about using her talents to move her staff members forward and make this world a better place for the students she serves:

Your life's purpose has a way of finding you, but not always in the way you would have ever expected it to. A career in education never crossed my thoughts, yet looking back, my talents for connection, personal growth, and the empowerment of others were being harnessed throughout my life experiences and the people I met along my journey.

I believe it takes the support, guidance, and leadership of others to help us not only recognize our talents, but to have the courage to use them in a way that leaves the world a better place. Our talents, whether innate or pursued, are the legacy we create, and in the words of Dave Burgess, "If what we're doing is powerful and could help other people, we have a moral imperative to share it." Knowing my talents allow others to shine, grow, and contribute to society fills my heart to the brim and consistently pushes me to step out of my comfort zone to use them for the betterment of our world.

The most powerful action we can take when looking to unleash the talents of others is to listen. Allow others to talk and look for that little spark of light that shows up in their eyes when something they are truly passionate about shines through. That right there is their life's purpose, and as an educator, I listen and watch for that moment so that I know where and how to support. Whether in the classroom or in a team meeting, our talents are what strengthen the dynamic, and I listen to understand, seek, and recognize everyone's strengths so that as a collective we can grow.

In the classroom, our class discussions allow me to observe and listen to learn who each and every one of my students is and what their talents are or could be. As a teacher, I am looked to as the expert in the room, which is something I dispel right away because I want my students to know that we are all constantly learning from one another. One group discussion I had a few years back was centered around learning, knowledge, and expertise in different areas. One of my students said, "Miss Ariss, you are the teacher. You are smarter than us." To which I replied, "I may know more things because I have had more life experience, but that doesn't mean I am smarter than you. You may have more experience than me in many areas, and because of that, you have a lot to teach me." I took this as an opportunity to refocus them on the concept we had discussed earlier: that every one of them had a talent, an area of strength, that could be shared with others. Creating and fostering a learning environment where students can unleash not only their own talents but the talents of others by working together, supporting one another, and implementing their strengths for the growth of others is transformational.

As educators, the more we share our talents, the more we empower others to share theirs. This extends beyond the classroom and into our school's culture. When we build a school community that is based on honoring and bringing forth the talents of its people, we create a place where everyone is safe, fulfilled, and striving for more. At a small rural school I worked at, I looked to my teaching partners as my family. We were all there for the same purpose, which was to ensure the best for the students in our care, and so each of us felt comfortable showing our vulnerability in sharing our areas of growth with one another. Each area of growth was someone else's area of strength, their talent, and by being open with one another, we were able to utilize our talents to build up the needs of others. This created a school where our students and families felt loved and welcomed, where they knew that trust bonded their teachers and that all of our unique talents were celebrated. This transformed our school from an institution to a home where everyone loved being every day.

The Bottom Line

It is in your hands to create a better world for all who live in it.

—**Nelson Mandela**

Transforming our schools begins with you and me. It begins with our colleagues down the hall and with those students who walk into our building every morning. As Sir Ken Robinson says, "Education can be encouraged from the top down but can only be improved from the ground up." Transformation is not merely an abstract concept; it is something that we all can take part in. Transformation begins—and will continue—as a direct result of our people. Our people can make or break school changes. Within each of our staff members and students are passions, skills, and personality traits that can bring hope, joy, light, and tremendous positive change to the field of education.

While we work diligently to make our schools better, it's important to tell our own stories, sharing our T3 with colleagues and students. When we work together to unleash the talent inside our schools, we are sending the message that every person matters every day. All talents, no matter how big or small or developed or mastered, are important. When people are valued for their passions, skills, and personality traits, there is no stopping us!

JOURNAL

Think about your school as a whole. What small things can you do within your day-to-day interactions with staff to help showcase talent?

_____

_____

_____

_____

_____

How can you help empower students to showcase their talents and the talents of their classmates as well?

_____

_____

_____

_____

_____

_____

DISCUSSION QUESTIONS

- Within your personal life or professional life, what brings out your color, and what drains it? How can you live more purposefully, in and out of school, to bring more color into your life and the lives of those you touch?

- When tapping into talents, how can we model and embed the importance and the art of practice? How can we give multiple chances for success, learning, and discomfort for staff members and students within our school day?

- What physiological or emotional barriers exist within your school and minds that get in your way to best leverage passion, skills, and traits? In which ways can you and others help eliminate these barriers?

- Within your role, how can you begin to better find and unleash the talents of the students you serve? Think of specific ideas and examples, no matter how big or small.

The meaning of life is
to find your gift.
The purpose of life is
to give it away.

William Shakespeare

CHAPTER 10

Talent Is Our Most Valuable Resource

*P*EOPLE ARE TRULY OUR most effective resource, and within our people exist talents that we must discover to fully understand and appreciate the individuals around us. If we view everyone as uniquely talented, we can begin to view people for the gifts they bring to the table rather than what they might lack. No one out there is exactly like anyone else, and what separates us is our T3: those passions, skills, and personality traits that make us who we are.

Philosopher Ralph Waldo Emerson said, "Make the most of yourself, for that is all there is of you." We were put on this earth for a reason, and it is our job to find it. Our talents and the talents that exist around us are too precious a resource to waste.

Talent as Electricity

Talent is like electricity.
We don't understand electricity.
We use it.

—MAYA ANGELOU

Maya Angelou's words are the perfect explanation of talent. Talent can be hard to define, but once it is experienced, it is understood. I like to think of our talents as electricity and our minds as the lightbulbs that contain it. If we can move past the roadblocks in our mind and use our talent, we can find our purpose.

Our talent is the spark that can make each and every other part of our life more meaningful. Our spark, just like electricity, gives us the energy to see the light that can help us find the way to keep going.

Electricity for our talent can begin in many sources and in many places, but ultimately we need to continue to be our own renewable resource that can find ways, times, and places to spark talent in our own lives and in the lives of others.

ELECTRICITY FOR OUR TALENT CAN BEGIN IN MANY SOURCES AND IN MANY PLACES, BUT ULTIMATELY WE NEED TO CONTINUE TO BE OUR OWN RENEWABLE RESOURCE THAT CAN FIND WAYS, TIMES, AND PLACES TO SPARK TALENT IN OUR OWN LIVES AND IN THE LIVES OF OTHERS.

One spark of inspiration and passion can be the beginnings of a beautiful collision in our lives where we can find value in the many talents we have to offer and share with others. Each of these sparks of electricity can help you find your blend of personality, passions, and skills that make you, you. How you ultimately find these talents and how you grow these talents in yourself and others can be a part of the mark you leave on the world.

Continuous Effort

My hope for you, your family, your colleagues, and your students is that you understand the importance of unleashing talent. Our gifts to the world are too important for us to lose interest in or to give up on. Once we find ways to grow our talent inside and outside of the workplace—and as we help others do the same—we have truly found our sweet spot. It's not easy. It takes continuous effort to identify, grow, and unleash talent. As writer Johann Wolfgang von Goethe said, "A really great talent finds its happiness in execution." In other words, finding a talent is not enough. One must act on the talent to really find bliss; therefore, find and utilize your talents now. Each day we are given is a gift, and this life is too short to take your own personal gifts for granted.

Stay true to your talents, but feel free to adapt them along the way as you discover new passions, skills, and personality traits. Use your T3 to make your school's culture more collaborative, diverse, and inclusive while also making those same efforts at home with family and friends. Together we can stand united for one purpose—to be the best we can be for each other and for students.

Talent Attracts Talent

*Don't judge each day
by the harvest you reap,
but by the seeds you plant.*
—**ROBERT LOUIS STEVENSON**

A few years ago, one of my mentors gave me this advice: Be so good at what you do in helping others grow that they eventually do not need you. Wow. What an absolutely beautiful and out-of-this-world perspective. It sounds absolutely terrifying—as far as job security goes—when you first hear it. But it makes sense, and this way of thinking is essential in empowering others in a way that will attract more talent long after you retire or shift roles.

Think of it this way: The talents that you now possess will be your gift to the world. Your talents can unleash talents in others that can outlast you, your career, your family, and future generations.

In other words, how can we unleash talents in all of us in a way that empowers staff and students now and in the future? It is an undeniably powerful thought and question. The seeds you plant and the small deeds you take part in to grow talent within others will amaze you. When you begin this journey and open your eyes to the talents around you, moments of amazement will happen more and more often in your day-to-day life.

THE TRUTH IS, OUR WORDS, TALENTS, AND OUR TIME HAVE THE POWER TO CHANGE ANOTHER PERSON'S LIFE FOR THE BETTER.

As an administrator, my days are always completely booked with meetings, evaluations, discipline, and the daily unexpected events you never foresee. To help unleash my T3, I take the time to help plant more tiny seeds of talents "on the edges" of any moment I can find. I love writing, and when I interact with students, I let them know they can send me their work, and I will coach them through any writer's block they might have. One of our students sent me an absolutely beautiful piece. I was completely blown away by her word choices, imagery, storytelling, and character development. In my feedback, I told her how much I loved it and that she should strongly consider becoming an author and self-publishing some of her work. A few months later, she emailed me to let me know that she had finished her piece and was taking my advice to self-publish. In her message, which made me cry, she shared how my belief in her talents was exactly what she needed to pursue her goals and to let her know she was indeed a great writer.

The truth is, our words, talents, and our time have the power to change another person's life for the better. Every moment matters, no matter how small. When we give others the room to shine, it can lead to the fulfillment of their talents. When it's unleashed, talent grows like a wildfire.

Talent > Fear

The people who are crazy enough to think they can change the world are the ones who do.

—**STEVE JOBS**

At times, I have come close to allowing my fear of failure and success to sabotage my dreams. I have also allowed the words of others or their potential opinions of me to get in my way and shift my thinking. As you move forward with your talents and embrace the talents of others, there will be people—sometimes even your own inner voice—who try to stop you or make you feel that you are not good enough. Keep in mind that your T3, your unique passions, skills, and personality traits, are greater than your fear.

Daring Greatly

It is not the critic who counts; not the man who points out how the strong man stumbles, or where the doer of deeds could have done them better. The credit belongs to the man who is actually in the arena, whose face is marred by dust and sweat and blood; who strives valiantly; who errs, who comes short again and again, because there is no effort without error and shortcoming; but who does actually strive to do the deeds; who knows great enthusiasms, the great devotions; who spends himself in a worthy cause; who at the best knows in the end the triumph of high achievement, and who at the worst, if he fails, at least fails while daring greatly.

A couple of years ago, I created this image based on an excerpt from what is arguably President Theodore Roosevelt's finest speech, "Citizenship in a Republic," (bit.ly/TRdaregreatly) on April 23, 1910, at the Sorbonne in Paris. This notable passage, originally shared more than one hundred years ago, remains just as powerful and moving today. When a message can touch generations, there must be a common thread that people can relate to time and time again.

Roosevelt's words are framed in my house and are a daily reminder to focus on action rather than fear. In general, we focus more on the critics and do not give enough thought and energy to the man in the arena or the individual evoking change. When you begin to embrace your talents and the talents of others, you might feel judged and critiqued. Rather than running away from your critics, face them; hear what they're saying, and learn when to embrace their assessments and when to dismiss them. Most importantly, focus the bulk of your energy on your own vision instead of on the opinions of others. Everyone feels inadequate at some point in life, but do not allow those fears to block your path. Be the one who keeps going, whose face is covered in dust, sweat, and blood, who falls short again and again but perseveres. Be the one in the arena.

What Trademark Will You Leave?

With each of your talents comes great responsibility. You have a responsibility to live the life you have always dreamed of. You have a responsibility to yourself and to others to use your talent for the greater good. None of us were meant to be common. We were born to be uncommon and uncommonly talented.

This world is counting on you to do so. It is never too late to leave your trademark. Your trademark is not just stamped on the world at the end of your life. It's left, for better or worse, each and every day. Your personal trademark is embedded into every person you meet. You have the choice every day to decide what your trademark will look like. It is up to you.

- Will you be the person that persevered to find and practice your potential talents even with the foreseen barriers?
- Will you be the person, the educator, the friend, the family member that was courageous enough to share their innate talents with others?
- Will you be the person that devoted their energies to unleash the talent in others, to help them reach their potential?
- Will you be the person that helped students feel so uncommonly talented that they could not help but also share their talents with the world?

NONE OF US WERE MEANT TO BE COMMON. WE WERE BORN TO BE UNCOMMON AND UNCOMMONLY TALENTED.

The Bottom Line

You must do the thing you think you cannot do.

—ELEANOR ROOSEVELT

Talent is not just one more thing. It is who you are. It is what you do. Talent is others. It is what they do. At the close of this book, I want you, the reader, to know the following:

I believe in you. I give you permission to be the talented person you are. Live your authentic life by being you and nobody else. Your skills, your personality traits, your passions, and each and every one of your T3 will do more than lift you up; they will change you and every single person around you. You are talented. This world is gifted by you, and you have gifts to share with the world—unique gifts that only you can share.

For my final send-off, I want to share with you some words that perfectly sum up all my hopes for you. On May 25, 2016, poet and educator Donovan Livingston delivered the graduation speech for the Harvard University Graduate School of Education. Here is my favorite part from his address:

> "... I've been a black hole in the classroom for far too long, absorbing everything without allowing my light to escape. But those days are done. I belong among the stars. And so do you. And so do they. Together, we can inspire galaxies of greatness for generations to come. No. The sky is not the limit. It is only the beginning. Lift off."

May you find ways to allow your light to escape every space within your life and your school so that you can unleash talent, joy, and love for years and years to come. Our staff members, students, families, and our future are depending on you. Go and do what you think you cannot do and take your talents and the talents of others to proudly and boldly unleash them to the world!

JOURNAL

How can you use your T3 talents to make your school, home, and world a better place? What can you begin to do tomorrow?

_____

_____

_____

_____

While reflecting and looking back at previous T3 goals that you listed while reading this book, which goal gives you the most fear to complete? Why?

_____

_____

_____

_____

_____

DISCUSSION QUESTIONS

- Within your school, how can you encourage others to be brave and be the man in the arena?

- When thinking of unleashing your own talents, which part of the process will be the most difficult for you to master? Why? What about unleashing talent in your staff members? Your students?

- How would you describe the current trademark that you leave with others? How would you shift or adapt the interactions you have with others to leave a trademark that better represents the legacy you want to leave?

- What specific things can you begin to do within your day-to-day life at school to better unleash your talent? The talent of others? The talent of students?

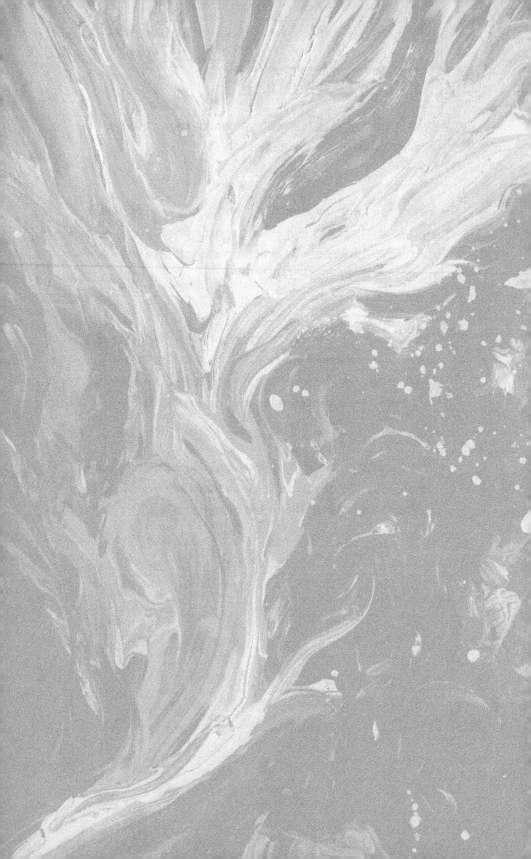

ACKNOWLEDGMENTS

First and foremost, I want to thank God. God, you are the ultimate provider of all gifts, talents, and life.

To my husband, Adam, who not only believes I can accomplish anything but always strives to be help me think differently. I love nothing more than being on the same team as you.

Last but not least, to the educators and colleagues who have shaped me and believed in me along the way. You have inspired me more than I could ever express. This book is for you.

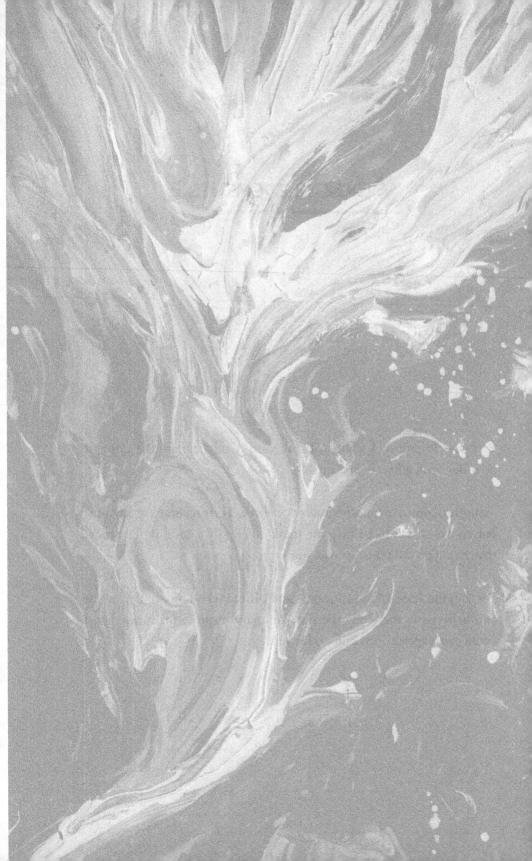

KEYNOTES AND WORKSHOPS

Kara Knollmeyer offers a variety of keynote presentations and workshops to help unleash talent in schools around the world. Learn more at karaknollmeyer.com/speaking.

UNLEASH TALENT FOR YOU, STAFF MEMBERS, TEACHERS, AND STUDENTS!

Talent is underrated. In our school systems, we see our students as talented, but often do not reflect those same thoughts when it comes to ourselves as adults. We often fail to recognize that we as staff members and teachers are the foundation of our school. Our talents, strengths, and passions are valuable and precious, just like our students. Just as we teach and reach the whole student, we need to teach and reach the whole adult. Therefore, we need to start finding, noticing, appreciating, embracing, and supporting the talents that our *adult* learners have. Not only will this radically change the school system by boosting teacher retention and happiness, but it will positively shift the way we interact and teach alongside students. No matter what your role is in education, we each have talents waiting to be awakened.

This keynote is based on Kara's book, *Unleash Talent: Bringing out the Best in Yourself and the Learners You Serve*. Based on what you or your group needs, this keynote/session can be centered on how to bring out the talent in all parties, or it can focus on a specific group: yourself, staff, teachers, or students!

DISCOVER YOUR T3
(Passions, Personality Traits, and Skills)

Dive into a guided session filled with learning, journaling, and deep self-reflection. Take a closer look to become one with your passions, personality traits, and skills by honing in on T3 you already have, while noticing new T3. In addition, before leaving the session, you will learn how you can personally use your T3 to live a more fulfilled life at school and at home!

TEAMING UP FOR T3

Every single person in our school system has T3 that are either untapped or could be taken to another level. How we approach our colleagues and acknowledge their unique strengths and abilities will form a direct correlation to true teamwork, collaboration, and unity. During this session, you will be guided with your teams to determine your own T3 and to learn about the specific talents of your team members. You will also be guided through team and reflection hands-on exercises to discover how to lift up one another by sharing your gifts with your colleagues and students.

SHOWCASE STUDENT TALENTS

Once we understand our own T3, how do we help our students bring our their own talents in their lives and in the school setting? Learn how to guide students into discovering their own T3. Explore practical and innovative ways to integrate the talents of your students into the school day to help make school a more purposeful place for each student who walks in our buildings.

CULTIVATING A POSITIVE SCHOOL CULTURE FOR TODAY, TOMORROW, AND YEARS TO COME

School culture is not one more thing to add it to your day; it is the essential piece that must be woven into everything we do. As staff members and leaders, we each have to take personal accountability for the energy we bring to the spaces we occupy—hallways, classrooms, and every inch of our building. Our values and actions have to match up in order for our culture to flourish. Whether we realize it or not, we each are currently setting either a positive or negative tone in our building—and those around us notice. In this session, you will learn the top habits of positive educators, how to use your talents to make school a better place for you and those around you, as well as many practical ideas to embed into your classroom and school. You will leave this session inspired to cultivate a positive school culture now, while making a meaningful trademark for years to follow.

DEVELOPING ENGAGING AND MEANINGFUL TEACHER PROFESSIONAL DEVELOPMENT

With teacher workloads heightening by the year, every minute of teacher professional development (PD) should be valued in gold! Learn how to purposefully build and organize a meaningful PD vision for your school (and how to adjust along the way), properly gain insight from staff members and stakeholders, and empower teachers and staff to lead based on their talents. Together, you'll discover how you can make progress on your school vision, mission, and purpose.

This session can be differentiated based on the specific PD needs of your building.

ENGAGE STUDENTS, STAFF, AND YOUR SCHOOL COMMUNITY WITH SOCIAL MEDIA

Are you wondering how you can use social media in your school or classroom? Would you like to take digital learning and sharing to the next level? This session offers an in-depth look at how to use social media in the classroom and school safely to engage students, families, and staff members in ways that will transcend learning! By gaining a focus and following simple strategies and ideas, you can get students and families even more excited about school, build endless connections with the world around you, and boost student learning and performance.

This session can be differentiated to focus on different social media platforms and can be catered to staff members, families, students, and/or school leaders.

TIPS AND TOOLS FOR ADMINISTRATOR EFFICIENCY:
How to Get the Biggest Bang for Your Buck so You Can Spend Less Time on Paperwork and More Time Making a Difference

If they aren't careful, administrators can drown in paperwork and menial tasks. It is crucial that, through our hectic and important days, we build ourselves for efficiency. Within this session, you will see ways to get the biggest bang for your buck, while regaining your sanity and happiness. You will learn about practical ideas, tools, and a multitude of resources I have created that have helped me, as a current administrator, spend more time on building relationships and making a difference, while spending less time on paperwork!

HOW DO I EVEN BLOG?

Blogging is a transformative way to reflect on your own learning, while connecting with the world around you. Learn my process for blogging: How I capture what inspires me, how I plan and make the time for blogging, and what tools and resources I use. By the end of this session, you will have a strong sense of how to blog professionally and personally. You'll also be able to transfer these skills and ideas for students.

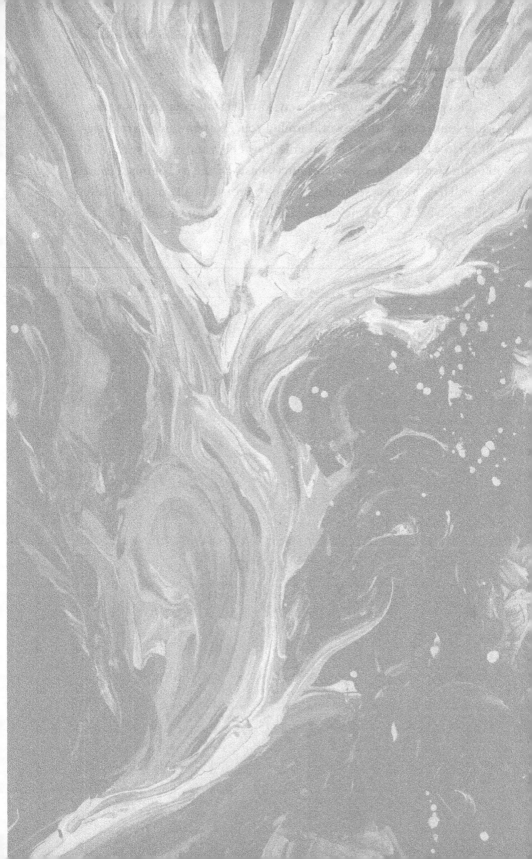

RESOURCES

CHAPTER 1

Fessler, Leah. "Completing this 30-minute exercise makes teams less anxious and more productive." *Quartz.* qz.com/1046131. Accessed June 21, 2018.

Reeves, Lynda. "Understanding Hard, Soft and Transferable Skills." San Diego Continuing Education. cds.sdce.edu/Assessment/Understanding-Skills. Accessed June 6, 2018.

Diener, Edward and Richard E. Lucas. "Personality Traits." *NOBA.* nobaproject.com/modules/personality-traits. Accessed June 6, 2018.

Pappas, Stephanie. "Personality Traits & Personality Types: What is Personality?" *Live Science.* September 7, 2017. livescience.com/41313-personality-traits.html. Accessed June 14, 2018.

CHAPTER 2

Kross, Ethan, et al. "Facebook Use Predicts Declines in Subjective Well-Being in Young Adults." *PLOS.* August 14, 2013. journals.plos.org/plosone/article?id=10.1371/journal.pone.0069841. Accessed June 14, 2018

Wagner, Philip. *Unlock Your Dream.* (New York, New York: Crown Publishing Group, 2016), page 16.

MacLean, David. "Don't be Content with Contentment." *Wholeheartedleaders.com.* March 18, 2015. wholeheartedleaders.com/cont-be-content-with-contentment. Accessed June 6, 2018.

Elle, Alexandra. *Words from a Wander.* (Create Space Independent Publishing Platform, 2013).

Brown, Brené. *Daring Greatly.*(New York, New York: Avery, 2012).

"Marie Curie Biography: Woman of Science." *Biographics.* January 25, 2018. biographics.org/marie-curie-biography-woman-of-science. Accessed June 6, 2018.

Polson, Jarrod and Wes Coker. *Living Beyond the Dream.* (Bloomington, Indiana: WestBow Press, 2015).

Epstein, David. *The Sports Gene.* (New York, New York: Current, 2013).

Eddie Cantor Biography. *IMDb.* imdb.com/name/nm0134662/bio. Accessed June 6, 2018.

Cardone, Grant. "The Gift of Obsession." *Entrepreneur.* December 10, 2015. entrepreneur.com/article/253737. Accessed June 6, 2018.

Landers, Ann. "Quotable Quote." *goodreads.* goodreads.com/quotes/ 279594-opportunities-are-usually-disguised-as-hard-work-so-most-people. Accessed June 14, 2018.

Williamson, Marianne. *Return to Love: Reflections on the Principles of a Course of Miracles.* (New York, New York: HarperCollins, 1992).

CHAPTER 3

Forleo, Marie. "Why You'll Never Find Your Passion." *Marie Forleo* blog. April 8, 2014. marieforleo.com/2014/04/find-your-passion. Accessed June 6, 2018.

Gordon, Jon. *The Carpenter.* (Hoboken, New Jersey: Wiley, 2014).

Mohr, Tara. *Playing Big.* (New York: New York: Avery, 2014).

Burgess, Shelley and Beth Houf, *Lead Like a PIRATE.* (San Diego, California: Dave Burgess Consulting, Inc., 2017).

Hurston, Zora Neale. *Dust Tracks on a Road.* (New York, New York: HarperCollins, 2006).

CHAPTER 4

DiSalvo, David. "Study: Receiving a Compliment has Same Positive Effect as Receiving Cash." *Forbes.* November 9, 2012. forbes.com/sites/ daviddisalvo/2012/11/09/study-receiving-a-compliment-has-same-positive-effect-as-receiving-cash/#3475d3c6007f. Accessed June 6, 2018.

Paine, Albert Bigelow. *Mark Twain, A Biography: The Personal and Literary Life of Samuel Langhorne Clemens, Volume 4.* (Harper & Brothers, 1912).

Staib, Karl. "5 Ways to Recognize and Utilize Talent." *Work Happy Now.* May 10, 2011. workhappynow.com/2011/05/5-ways-to-recognize-and-utilize-talent. Accessed June 6, 2018.

"Grassley Continues Efforts to Help Gifted and Talented Students and Educators." Chuck *Grassley United States Senator for Iowa.* March 2, 2005. grassley.senate.gov/ news/news-releases/grassley-continues-efforts-help-gifted-and-talented-students-and-educators-1. Accessed June 6, 2018.

CHAPTER 5

Burgess, Shelley and Beth Houf, *Lead Like a PIRATE.* (San Diego, California: Dave Burgess Consulting, Inc., 2017).

Olave, Becca. "Keeping the Romance Alive AFTER Kids." *The Dating Divas.* September 10, 2016. thedatingdivas.com/10-ways-to-keep-the-romance-alive-after-kids. Accessed June 6, 2018.

Sivers, Derek. "Obvious to You, Amazing to Others" YouTube video. Posted June 28, 2011. youtube.com/watch?v=xcmI5SSQLmE. Accessed June 6, 2018.

Wiliam, Dylan. "Understanding the Role of the Professional in Sustaining Change ." TeachingCouncil.ie. March 7, 2015. teachingcouncil.ie/en/Publications/ Promoting-Teaching/Education-Papers/Understanding-the-Role-of-the-Professional-in-Sustaining-Change.pdf. Accessed June 6, 2018.

CHAPTER 7

Brownn, Eleanor. "Self-Care Is Not Selfish." *EleanorBrownn.com.* November 2, 2014. eleanorbrownn.com/blog2/self-care-in-not-selfish. Accessed June 6, 2018.

"David Allen on How to Be Present in the Moment." *London Real* YouTube video. May 14, 2015. youtube.com/watch?v=anWT7ciskNA. Accessed June 6, 2018.

Williams, Pat. *How to Be Like Coach Wooden.* (Deerfield Beach, Florida: Heath Communications, 2006).

Sinek, Simon. *Start with Why.* (New York, New York: Penguin, 2009).

Brown, Brené. *Daring Greatly.*(New York, New York: Avery, 2012).

Weinstein, Matt. "How to Have More Fun in Your Life." *TEDx Talks.* Livermore, January 20, 2015. youtu.be/TXwH3SIF9rc. Accessed June 6, 2018.

CHAPTER 8

Rusche, Bryan. "Why You Need to Give Your Employees Feedback & How to Do It." *SOAPBOX*. soapboxhq.com/blog/management-skills/giving-employee-feedback. Accessed June 6, 2018.

Sandberg, Sheryl. *Lean In*. (New York, New York: Knopf, 2013).

Bryant, Adam. "Diane von Furstenberg: The Key to Success Is Trusting Yourself." *New York Times*. May 3, 2015. nytimes.com/2015/05/03/business/ diane-von-furstenberg-the-key-to-success-is-trusting-yourself.html. Accessed June 6, 2018.

CHAPTER 9

Lara, Daniel Martínez and Rafa Cano Méndez. *Alike*, a short film. (Spain: Daniel Martínez Lara & La Fiesta P.C., 2016).

Coyle, Daniel. *The Talent Code*. (New York, New York: Bantam Dell, 2006).

Robinson, Ken, and Lou Aronica. *Creative Schools*. (New York, New York: Penguin, 2015).

CHAPTER 10

Wood, James. *Dictionary of Quotations from Ancient and Modern English and Foreign Sources*. (London: Frederick Waren and Co.,1893).

Roosevelt, Theodore. "Citizenship in a Republic." Speech delivered at the Sorbonne in Pairs, France. April 23, 1910.

Livingston, Donovan. Harvard Graduate School of Education Student Speech. *Harvard Education*. May 25, 2016. youtube.com/watch?v=9XGUpKITeJM. Accessed June 6, 2018.

More From

IMPRESS

Empower
What Happens When Student Own Their Learning

By A.J. Juliani and John Spencer

In an ever-changing world, educators and parents must take a role in helping students prepare themselves for anything. That means unleashing their creative potential! In *Empower*, **A.J. Juliani** and **John Spencer** provide teachers, coaches, and administrators with a roadmap that will inspire innovation, authentic learning experiences, and practical ways to empower students to pursue their passions while in school.

Learner-Centered Innovation
Spark Curiosity, Ignite Passion, Unleash Genius

By Katie Martin

Learning opportunities and teaching methods must evolve to match the ever-changing needs of today's learners. In *Learner-Centered Innovation*, **Katie Martin** offers insights into how make the necessary shifts and create an environment where learners at every level are empowered to take risks in pursuit of learning and growth rather than perfection.

ABOUT THE AUTHOR

KARA KNOLLMEYER is a wife, daughter, sister, and administrator in St. Louis, Missouri. An award-winning educational leader, Kara has been recognized for her contributions to the educational field. In 2017, Kara received the Midwest Spotlight Educator (METC) Award. She also received the Missouri Outstanding Beginning Teacher Award (Missouri Association of Colleges for Teacher Education) in 2013.

Her journey through elementary and secondary education has included experiences as a teacher, language arts team leader, new teacher district facilitator, language arts and social studies curriculum writer, and a mentor teacher. Currently, Kara serves as a middle school assistant principal.

Kara believes everyone has unique gifts that should be shared with the world. Her mission is to empower people to unleash the talent within themselves and others. She believes that uplifting everyone within the school community can ignite a culture of purpose where the strengths of all learners—adults and children alike—are celebrated.

CONNECT WITH KARA

Blog: karaknollmeyer.com
Twitter: @karaknollmeyer

UnleashTalentBook.com
Post your learning and connect with the community of learners
using the hashtag #UnleashTalent on Twitter and social media!